MASTERS AT WORK

MASTERS AT WORK

BECOMING A TEACHER

MELINDA D. ANDERSON

SIMON & SCHUSTER

New York   London   Toronto   Sydney   New Delhi

Simon & Schuster
1230 Avenue of the Americas
New York, NY 10020

First Simon & Schuster hardcover edition September 2020

SIMON & SCHUSTER and colophon are registered trademarks
of Simon & Schuster, Inc.

For information about special discounts for bulk purchases,
please contact Simon & Schuster Special Sales at 1-866-506-1949
or business@simonandschuster.com.

The Simon & Schuster Speakers Bureau can bring authors to
your live event. For more information or to book an event, contact
the Simon & Schuster Speakers Bureau at 1-866-248-3049
or visit our website at www.simonspeakers.com.

Illustrations by Donna Mehalko

Manufactured in the United States of America

3 5 7 9 10 8 6 4

Library of Congress Cataloging-in-Publication Data has been applied for.

ISBN 978-1-9821-3990-2
ISBN 978-1-9821-3991-9 (ebook)

I celebrate teaching that enables transgressions—
a movement against and beyond boundaries.
It is that movement which makes education the practice of freedom.

—bell hooks

CONTENTS

BECOMING
A TEACHER

INTRODUCTION

O ver fifty million children return to America's public school classrooms every year. Across over 98,000 schools in some 13,600 local school districts, spanning big cities, small towns, and rural communities across the country. More than any other public institution, schools transmit the norms and values that underpin and define Americanness—chiefly through students' daily contact with our nation's more than three million public school teachers. This book tells the story of one master teacher in the enormous, messy, and complex system of American public schooling.

Entire volumes have been written about teaching. In its purest form, teaching hinges on the connection between one teacher and dozens—or even hundreds—of students. How does a teacher set academic goals and move them forward? How does a lesson unfold? How much of teaching is improvisation? How can what occurs in a classroom transform a child's sense of self and value outside of school? Here you will encounter the nitty-gritty of the profession. From an unconventional path to the classroom and licensure struggles, to an eye-opening rookie year, the tenacity required in the early years, and the path toward mastery. The less glamorous parts of teaching, and the unique experiences of Black teachers, round out the story.

When LaQuisha Hall arrived in Baltimore in 2003, she was twenty-one, recently transplanted from North Carolina, and a fresh-faced hire as an English teacher in Baltimore's public schools. Her seventeen-year career in Charm City is dotted with stints in Baltimore middle and high schools, including a yearlong assignment at the city's alternative school for students removed from neighborhood schools.

Hall is an artist; a life coach; a pageant winner; and an advocate for sexual assault survivors. Every piece of her identity funnels into her teaching. For close to two decades, she has conceived and carried out creative, empowering, and culturally responsive lessons that sharpen students' reading, writing, and life skills—resulting in her selection as the 2018 Baltimore City Schools Teacher of the Year.

Her school, Carver Vocational-Technical High School, is a supporting actor in the story. Named after the famous Black inventor George Washington Carver, it was founded in 1925 as a vocational school for Black students during the era of de jure school segregation. Today the school prepares its nearly entirely Black student body for certifications in a

variety of trades, including cosmetology, carpentry and electrical construction, and food and beverage management. A separate program (P-TECH) creates a pathway for students to graduate high school with a diploma and a two-year associate's degree. The school is a fixture in the city, with its revered history and generations of graduates living in and around Baltimore.

I am a product of public schools with conscientious and committed teachers. But none stood out from the rest. I benefited from the education I received. But teaching is much more than pouring facts into a child's head. Here is a portrait of a dynamic, unforgettable teacher who is making an indelible mark on the young people she serves, as I observed firsthand in the 2018–19 and 2019–20 school years—comprising her sixteenth and seventeenth years in teaching. What follows is also a scrutinizing look at the system in which she works that contributes to the larger conversation about the state of public education.

Modeling the best of her profession, Hall is a springboard to enlighten and bring clarity to a very much maligned and misunderstood job. Spotlighting teaching's wonders and warts serves as a primer for aspiring teachers, an affirmation for current teachers, and a wake-up call for those who care about sustaining this noble profession.

1

COUNTDOWN

Gray clouds hang low over Carver Vo-Tech High School in the closing weeks of the school year. Here in West Baltimore's Coppin Heights neighborhood, neatly maintained homes and boarded-up rowhouses coexist in a community that boasts a heavy police presence, but not one major chain supermarket or bookstore. Coppin Heights stands in sharp contrast to the Inner Harbor, Baltimore's showpiece—a tourist attraction a few miles away on the waterfront. Carver Vo-Tech is the prototypical urban high school: a sprawling redbrick structure, towering over the nearby buildings and engulfing the entire corner. The front office greets visitors with WELCOME TO CARVER, HOME OF THE BEARS opposite a barren foyer that houses an un-manned metal detector. LaQuisha Hall, smiling brightly, swings open the door, fluid and playful in a flowing sum-mer dress of emerald green, navy blue, and orange, with gold-streaked Senegalese twist braids. She is cheerful, her loose ponytail swinging as the call-and-response of "Good morning, Mrs. Hall!" "Good morning, queen!" "How are you, king?" is repeated. The route to her classroom is an obstacle course, weaving through slow-moving youngsters in blue polo shirts and khaki pants, the Carver school uniform. The long hallway—adorned with inspirational quotes from Henry Ford, William Butler Yeats, and Margaret Mead—is a throwback to a more staid era.

That feeling is dashed rounding the corner to room 263. Vibrant drawings of African masks cover the classroom's wooden door and glass block windows. The entrance is a tribute to Harlem Renaissance artist and educator Loïs Mailou Jones from a Black Baltimore teacher who always dreamed of being a professional artist. Passing through the doorway, Hall's artistic flourishes blend with an unapologetic atmosphere of Black excellence. The Western canon of dead white male poets is scuttled in favor of Maya Angelou's poem

"Phenomenal Woman" hanging as a poster that deconstructs the work's themes of female empowerment. Neon-blue bins filled with young adult novels by some of the hottest Black and Latinx writers—Elizabeth Acevedo, Jason Reynolds, Daniel José Older, Angie Thomas, and Baltimore native Kwame Alexander—sit on a windowsill below Langston Hughes's jarring poem "A Dream Deferred." Standard markings of a high school English classroom surround the space: vocabulary words, the rules for literature circles, and a handwritten sign nudging readers to practice critical thinking.

The attention to detail signals that this is a place where the teacher's work goes beyond academics, and beyond the classroom. Sitting at home the last weekend in May 2019, Hall scrolled Facebook and saw that hundreds of teens had gathered at the Inner Harbor on a warm Saturday night. As media reports of a "juvenile disturbance" flooded in, all Hall could think about were her clever and sweet-spirited freshmen at Carver who had celebrated the publication of their first book days before. She had heavily promoted the book event to local TV stations and media outlets, but not one news camera or reporter showed up. Now they were giving events at the Inner Harbor breaking-news coverage. Hall was personally offended by the persistent drumbeat denigrating young, Black Baltimore residents. So she went rogue on her Facebook page, posting photos of the book signing and demanding the media report on the students at Carver Vo-Tech to give context and meaning to the larger story of Baltimore youth.

But more than the sensational headlines and exaggerated reporting disturbed her. Hall is not naive to the perils of being young and Black in Baltimore. She has lost students to incarceration and tragic deaths—an unwelcome though not uncommon consequence of teaching in an urban school district—and suspected some of her impressionable ninth-graders were at the Inner Harbor. She decided to use the incident in her classroom to encourage her students to make smart, lifesaving choices outside Carver's walls this summer: "I'm not just going to give them work to do. I want them to work on themselves. I really want them to think 'Maybe I shouldn't go with that friend, because she's always up to no good' to prevent me from losing more kids." The sober reality is that West Baltimore can be a crushing place to be a Black teen. Many years of ingrained, systemic racism has led to entrenched inequalities in social services, housing, and job opportunities. It's a neighborhood afflicted with a high rate of violence and crime due to decades of economic disinvestment and generational poverty. Hall's optimism may be premature. But fighting hard for her kids, the only children she has, isn't impulsive. It's intentional. A hallmark of her teaching practice that's been finely calibrated over the last sixteen years—her entire career spent in the Baltimore City Schools.

In room 263, young ladies are "queens," young men are "kings," and scholars excel. Hall adopted the terms several years ago to help her kids internalize the importance of being confident, curious, lifelong learners. Aiming to give every child a chance to shine, she initiated the "Scholars of the Week" recognition. Initially she handed out monthly honors, but as is common in teaching, Hall reconsidered. "I wondered if the kids that I didn't highlight had ever heard anything good about themselves," she said. "I wanted them all by the end of the school year to say, 'Mrs. Hall thinks that I can write,' so they don't turn into that adult that says, 'No teacher ever told me anything good about myself.'" The payoff was immediate and dramatic: students came to class every Monday, excited to learn who would be chosen, reveling in the attention. Joy is an undervalued and overlooked element in our culture and schools. The drive for high test scores can dwarf the simple satisfaction that comes from a teacher creating an environment where everyone is acknowledged, not just top-performing students. Creating a sense of belonging carries over into how students see themselves as learners. In the pressure cooker of the classroom joy can seem like a luxury, but it's as vital as a well-constructed syllabus.

As youngsters file into English 1, exchanging banter with Hall, the quirkiness of ninth-graders is apparent: equal parts cocky and cynical, curious and cautious, selfish and selfless. Hall scribbles questions on the dry-erase board to introduce her lesson on the Inner Harbor episode as they take their seats. She will rely on a teaching approach passed down from Greek philosophers—the Socratic method, with students leading their own learning through inquiry-based dialogue. In preparation for today's discussion, Hall assigned a reading on Kalief Browder, a New York City teen who was accused of stealing a backpack in 2010. The sixteen-year-old was sent to Rikers Island, one of America's most brutal prisons, and incarcerated for nearly three years while awaiting trial on the charges. Her students learn that the trauma he suffered in jail was a major cause of his later suicide. Hall draws parallels to the take-home reading with a brief clip on the Central Park Five from *CBS News Sunday Morning*. Similar to Browder, it is a chilling example of racial profiling that resulted in young Black and Latino teens being falsely accused and wrongfully convicted of a heinous crime. Hall asks how many of her students are watching *When They See Us*, a Netflix miniseries about the infamous 1989 case. As hands go up, she tells them to write down their thoughts from the news segment, and points to the Socratic seminar topics on the board.

What are your thoughts on what happened to Browder? The Central Park Five? How are they the same/different?

How do these cases relate to issues occurring in Baltimore?

Think about the recent Inner Harbor incident. What ways can Black youth protect themselves? What other things can Baltimore youth do this summer? What other places can they go?

A troop of students saunters to chairs placed in the center of the room, as classmates shift seats for a better view. "Diamond," animated in cornrows and glasses, initiates the conversation, making the connection between Browder, the Central Park Five, and Black teens like themselves. "At the Inner Harbor, they called us criminals," she says. "On Netflix, the cops called them animals." The discourse reveals the scholars' unfiltered selves—the spirit of Socrates with some stank on it. With the energy running high, the students switch places. But the second group can't find its rhythm. Diamond, now seated on the outside, asks Hall if she can help them. She encourages the young girl's enthusiasm and reminds her of the Socratic process—those inside the circle speak, those outside the circle listen and respond. Skillful facilitation by Hall, giving prompts and validating their experiences, sparks a discussion bursting with honesty and raw emotion: "They don't see us either—nothing positive"; "My brother's going to have to do time again, 5–10 years, for just being in the wrong place at the wrong time"; and "The whole entire system is corrupt." With the class period ending, Diamond lights up, finally able to say what she's been holding inside. Racing to finish before the bell sounds, she leaves her classmates with a piece of shrewd and cautionary advice: "Be a leader, not a follower!"

Much is made of bringing the real world into classrooms. It can be done poorly, with teachers making perfunctory attempts at including current events—or it can be done well, with teachers aligning the content to students' lived experiences, and guiding students to make connections between the news and themselves. Providing a forum for young people to read, write, and ruminate on biases and stereotypes that afflict Black youth packs an especially heavy punch on the fourth anniversary of Browder's death. Hall, settled at her desk, recounting the just-completed session, has watched her scholars bloom through Socratic seminars, which she introduced midyear. "When you have a conversation in a classroom, even when the kids raise their hand and they're called on, somebody might yell out an answer right before they say it. But this is so focused and methodical." The strategy is a way to meet the state standards for freshman English, and an opportunity to slip in a life skill many adults lack. Inside the circle "they're utilizing the Common Core skills of compare and contrast, as students on the outside are listening," she says, emphasizing the importance of her scholars learning "to stop and hear what someone else is saying and consider the other side."

Whether formally teaching English language arts or informally strolling the school's corridors, she is present in the moment. Walking the halls before her next class, she eyes two girls by the door of the vo-tech high school's cosmetology studio. Hall smoothly links arms with one young lady and escorts her down the hallway as her pal shuffles behind them. In whispered tones she shares how to be a supportive friend when it's not reciprocated, and the necessity to love some people from afar, in a tender voice filled with reassurance. The listener nods and smiles, as her buddy—Hall's one-person amen corner—approvingly seconds all of the guidance. Hall is auntie, big sis, counselor, and confidante. Essentially, the person she desperately needed in the turbulence of her own adolescence.

A survivor of family domestic violence and childhood sexual abuse by a relative, Hall struggled with the emotional fallout from early childhood through her teens in New Bern, North Carolina. After high school graduation, she headed to Elizabeth City State University, a small historically Black college in a rural community on North Carolina's coast. But along with the décor for her dorm room, she carried the trauma and scars from New Bern into her freshman year, culminating in a suicide attempt. Gradually, she found healing and deliverance in the church, and channeled years of pain into uplifting and encouraging others, like the children in room 263 and former students she sees in the hallways at Carver.

Hall's origin story guides her life and her teaching—in ways that some of her colleagues don't understand. "When I talk to other teachers about my plans and ideas, they call it over-the-top," she says. "You're not required to publish students in a book. But I want them to feel they are heard and seen, unlike me growing up. Not enough was done for me . . . now I'm in a position to offer what I didn't have." In her role as a Baltimore City teacher, Hall rallies her scholars to "reach their greatness and meet their full potential," adding "God allowed me to overcome a whole lot of hardship so I could help a whole lot of other people." She is driven by a tenacious desire to create a classroom where trust and safety are the values that bolster the academic mission.

Her success in this pursuit is evident during a class period late in the day as kids sit quietly for independent reading. The sound of pages turning is broken by yelling. A fight is underway in the hallway outside room 263. As the cacophony of youthful voices and adult reprimands grows outside, the readers inside Hall's quiet cavern never look up. The astounding focus is modeled by Hall, who projects calm and composure in the midst of chaos only feet away. "I've never said to them that if there's a fight, you cannot run to my door," she explains. "But they know I'm not going to let anyone come in this class and harm them. Once I established that no one would come in here and hurt them . . . they felt safe. Whatever's happening in the hallway right now is not going to affect them."

Rather than a simplistic platitude, "students can't learn if they don't feel safe" speaks to the physical and emotional well-being that is a precondition for students to learn. School shootings and ICE immigration raids, among other threats, have struck fear into children, leaving teachers to manage their anxieties and trauma. This is particularly acute for Black children, who experience an "alarming rate of exposure to violence and victimization," according to data from the National Center for Victims of Crime. There is clearly a need for more mental health professionals in schools. Yet in their absence, teachers like Hall fill the void, prioritizing care before composition.

The final bell buzzes and Carver falls silent, a stream of students and staff passing through the exit. Hall sinks into her chair, that morning's half-finished venti cinnamon dolce latte still on her desk. Today's instruction was fueled by caffeine, chips, and fruit snacks—not an infrequent occurrence. Asked if she relishes being one day closer to the end of the school year, she rejects the rush to bring the curtain down on her scholars.

Candidly, she laments that bidding farewell to this class of freshmen will be tough. She proudly stares at three sheets of flip chart paper with a satisfied smile. The detailed inventory, titled "Keeping up with Mrs. Hall Scholars," records all of the authors they met, museums they visited, work they created, and projects they executed. Nearly 100 percent of her students started the school year as reluctant readers—by the end of the year, those same students had collectively read 190 books—more than 68,000 pages; written and published a book; and celebrated their reading accomplishments with a party bus trip to Pizza Hut. She will wait until after the students are gone to pack up her room, savoring what was.

In the interim, she and her coworkers participate in the annual ritual known as the end-of-year teacher luncheons. On two consecutive days during the last week of school, Carver staff members are feted with a southern buffet of collard greens, chicken, and mashed potatoes, along with a Maryland crab feast. At the Carver cookout Hall is hailed as a "High Achiever" for "Thinking Out of the Box." As the festivities wane, she concedes that the custom of year-end teacher meals and recognitions, while genuinely appreciated, is poorly timed: "When I'm a little sluggish— when I was hungry and had to teach—that's when I needed that lunch to say, 'Hey, we see you, keep going!' And it'd be nice to know that you thought I was a high achiever on the days I didn't feel high achieving. That gratitude should be shown to us all year, not at the end." Back in her classroom, she pushes aside disapproving judgments, quickly pivoting to her scholars—the solid relationships they built and how much they soared.

"I really loved my students this year," she says, resigned to the reality she'll have to pass them on to another teacher. "They did a lot of stuff that I would have liked to have done with other students in the past." That includes a classroom yearbook in which all fifty-eight of her 2018–19 freshmen shared their favorite lesson and cherished moment from her class, as well as advice about Hall's class for delivery to next year's incoming scholars. She clutches the notebook with a mixture of affection and reverence: "If they don't get anything from the curriculum of Baltimore City Schools, I want them to know that they have to be more than what is expected of them. If they can put it in their own words without my prompting, I feel like I did my job. And I know that I did that with these students this year."

2

PATH TO THE CLASSROOM

The poster with script lettering hangs behind Hall's desk as a daily affirmation: "I became a teacher because your life is worth my time." The mantra, fierce and decisive, is striking, given how she came to be a teacher—a story rooted more in chance than intent. Hall was filled with indecision as she approached graduation from Elizabeth City State University in the spring of 2003. The English major had squeaked into law school at Regent University, a Christian school in Virginia Beach, Virginia, with a middling LSAT score, triggering doubts about her future in the legal field. With her eyes set on graduate school, a friend told Hall about a federally funded program called Project Site Support. The pitch was enticing: receive a tuition-free master's degree at Baltimore's Morgan State University in exchange for a five-year salaried teaching stint in the city's public schools. The reality was startling: recruits would earn their master's degree while teaching full-time in Baltimore—arriving by July, leading a classroom solo by September.

Hall had never considered teaching and had never been to Baltimore. Living independently from her parents, she was barely getting by in college on a part-time job at CVS. The idea of a no-cost graduate degree and a starting salary of some $35,000 was very tempting. Weighing her options between a career in education or law, her selection was dictated by a certain pragmatism. "I ended up choosing [teaching] because I wanted to be able to continue working and take care of myself," she confessed.

The decision put her on an unconventional path. Teachers traditionally start by obtaining a four-year bachelor's degree from a school of education. But a declining number of education majors and persistent teacher shortages had spurred states to act by endorsing accelerated pathways into teaching. About 18 percent of public school teachers entered through an alternative track in 2015–16, with a greater number of Black, Hispanic, and male teachers choosing this method over traditional teacher-training programs. Although every state's requirements differ, alternative routes generally allow candidates with a bachelor's degree to pursue an expedited path to teacher licensure, also known as certification. Hall's nontraditional route was part of a growing trend, creating more avenues for those who had not completed education coursework and groups under-represented in the teacher workforce.

Project Site Support, announced with great fanfare in the fall of 1999, pledged to recruit and prepare 1,400 new teachers for Maryland's toughest-to-staff schools. Among the individuals in Hall's cohort of newbies was a researcher, a financial advisor, a bank auditor—and, as a fluke, a lawyer. The initiative, funded with a $12.6 million, five-year grant from the U.S. Department of Education, was a collaboration between three Baltimore-area colleges that boldly promised "a new generation of urban teachers." By the fall of 2003, when Hall started teaching, the government-funded effort had made serious inroads into Baltimore City Schools: one-third of the teachers hired that school year had come through the program, and it claimed an 85 percent teacher retention rate.

Hall was oblivious to the culture shock that awaited her in Baltimore. It was her first trip outside North Carolina. As she rode north in a U-Haul truck, leafy green landscapes transformed into rows of attached houses, signaling her arrival in a post-industrial city with dual identities—a white Baltimore that brags of urban renewal, and a majority-Black Baltimore mired in a legacy of neglect and discrimination.

Being on the campus of Morgan State, Maryland's largest historically Black university, felt familiar, but nothing else did. Her southern upbringing seemed an impediment to meeting new people and making connections, causing her to question herself and her choice. Back home, she would greet strangers on the street; in Baltimore, "they would roll their eyes and suck their teeth or ask, 'What are you looking at?'" The reception from classmates within her preparation program was also chilly, and socially she felt isolated as "the little Christian girl who couldn't go drinking and dancing" with her peers.

She channeled her discontent into her studies, balancing the teaching grind with her master's in secondary education. Project Site Support vowed that its faculty and staff would help the recruits transition into teaching. But for Hall, the guidance was lacking. "It was more of a gripe session," she recollects, with class periods spent processing the graduate students' complaints about their grueling days, rather than giving the novices meaningful instruction and support. Analysis of alternative certification programs has under-scored their strengths and weaknesses. Ardent supporters cite the need for teachers in hard-to-staff school districts, and the desire of many aspiring teachers to bypass the time-honored teacher preparation route. Critics point to the pitfalls of an add-water-and-stir approach to teacher prep, with evidence that fast-tracked teachers feel less prepared and are more likely to quit.

Before embarking on this new career, Hall had never thought about what it takes to be a good teacher. The classes at Morgan State were designed to provide the knowledge and technical abilities that, with practice, would equip her for the classroom. The courses checked the boxes that needed to be checked. Effective teaching, like all professions, is a fusion of talents and competencies, among them exceptional oral and verbal communication skills; attentiveness to others' needs; unending patience and resourcefulness; stellar organization and time management; and a reservoir of motivation. "I envisioned teaching was nothing more than go in a classroom, share a lesson, and grade their papers," she says. "No one ever said—sometimes you're going to have to let your hair down, be a little compassionate, even if that child comes late every single day." So the neophyte looked to her prior educators for strength and inspiration.

From her high school AP English teacher, Hall learned the significance of encouragement and acceptance. Mrs. Futrell helped her demystify the written word, analyzing books that Hall found confusing. Most memorably, she invited Hall to an end-of-school-year cookout at her house. It was Hall's white English teacher who made her feel accomplished and welcomed when she felt that all of the kids in the class were so much smarter than her—and as one of the few Black students, she felt that she didn't belong. She jokes that when Futrell, now a Facebook friend, likes her posts, she rereads them to make sure they are grammatically correct.

She holds the same admiration for her freshman English professor at Elizabeth City State. Hall recalls Dr. Griffin asking the class who had read *Invisible Man*, Ralph Ellison's seminal novel—and her dismay when not one Black student in her class, at a historically Black university, raised their hand. Griffin broke down crying, imploring her Black students to read the book and know its themes of race, racism, and inequality in America. Hall was shook. "I could feel the hurt even behind the tears. I could feel her spirit diminish," she said. "I'd never seen a teacher care, not like that, about me reading a particular book." She read *Invisible Man*, and eventually added it to her own teacher bookshelf. "I don't want my students to ever say 'I never heard of it,' which was my answer at the time." Griffin forever changed her relationship to literature and taught her the relevance of exposure in teaching Black youth—a critical bridge to her high school students in Baltimore.

As she pulled wisdom from her past, and took stock of

her skills, the decision was settled: she would work in a large, urban school system, and teach high school English. Teaching elementary school or getting certified in special education would require additional schooling, and she was already carrying substantial student loan debt from her undergraduate degree. Choosing Project Site Support predetermined her early career options. Unlike most new teachers, Hall never had to chew over basic choices like where to work, or grade level or subject to teach, all of which require thoughtful consideration.

Deciding where to work is a major one. Headlines have long proclaimed a national shortage of qualified teachers. Yet a May 2016 report by the nonpartisan Education Commission of the States (ECS), a Colorado-based education policy center, found insufficient evidence "to support claims of an increasing teacher shortage on a national level." What persists, writes ECS, are localized shortages within states; perennial shortfalls in specific subjects—such as math, science, and special education—that are exacerbated by colleges of education overproducing candidates in low-demand areas like elementary education; and chronic shortages in urban and rural schools, as well as schools concentrated with poverty and students of color. Additionally, the ability of teachers to move to where the jobs are is hampered by state policies that restrict their mobility—ECS discovered in 2017 that only six states (Arizona, Florida, Hawaii, Mississippi, Missouri, and Nevada) offer full reciprocity to fully licensed out-of-state teachers.

Settling on a grade level or content area also necessitates reflection and planning. Veteran educator Vanessa Dodo Seriki, an associate professor at Morgan State University, said prospective elementary teachers gain a generalist's education in fields ranging from science, to social studies, to music and math. Most elementary education majors she's worked with also had a zeal for teaching young children. Which is a prized attribute, she says, given elementary teachers spend the entire day with the same group of kids: "Being the mother of four children, those are the kind of people you want working with younger children—people who have a passion for it." Similarly, she finds teachers who choose to go into secondary education are driven by their strong interest in specific subject areas, like history, biology, foreign languages, or English, and a preference for teaching older, distinct groups of students.

Especially complex is special education, in which teachers must deliver individualized instruction based on the unique needs of students with disabilities. Regardless of a teacher-in-training's specialty, the curriculum in teacher education requires all budding educators to be grounded in diverse courses of study—from human development, psychology, and methods for teaching particular content, to disciplines like history and sociology. Typically, schools of education also require at least one class in classroom management and multicultural education, a necessary but insufficient prerequisite, said Dodo Seriki, who is herself a former Baltimore high school science teacher. Ideally, new teachers enter the classroom steeped in the pedagogical knowledge about how people learn, ready to translate theory into practice.

What teacher education has not perfected, however, is identifying the dispositions beginning teachers should have before walking into classrooms. Such as genuinely liking young people, Dodo Seriki stressed, and not as an empty cliché, but caring enough to build positive, attentive relationships. Students accepted into education school should have an allegiance to social justice, or as she says more plainly, "No matter if they're [teaching] in urban schools or in rural schools, they should have a commitment to value what students bring to the classroom . . . the diversity that exists." The majority of public school students in America are now kids of color.

As Dodo Seriki confirms, many educators enter the classroom without a full grasp of what constitutes being a teacher, and the intangibles needed to be successful. This is the case even with student teaching, when preservice teachers pilot test with real kids what they have learned in teacher training, while supervised by an experienced master teacher. There is simply no substitute for standing in the front of a classroom with sole responsibility for motivating and educating other people's children.

Hall felt unprepared on her first day, and it had nothing to do with her lesson plan. Stylishly dressed in a suit, she looked the part. She was counseled not to tell the kids her age, but it didn't matter. She was a young-looking twenty-one-year-old, and knew her students "could smell fresh meat." Her lack of seasoning was apparent. She admits she might have been too lax about tardiness and behavior, telegraphing to her students that anything goes. "They started asking, 'Did you just start teaching?' I wanted them to have fun, but not the kind of fun that they were anticipating."

It was the basics on how to conduct herself the first day so that the rest of her school year went smoothly that tripped her up. Like many teachers, her most valuable lessons were learned on the job through trial and error. "My first day should have sounded more like, 'I understand you're late today, because everybody is trying to find their classroom, but please know, there's a policy.' I didn't reinforce those things [because] I didn't know the importance of it at that time."

When Hall finally found her rhythm, her full-time teaching schedule was complicated by the demands of studying for her teaching license exam. In Maryland, like many other states, teachers must pass the *Praxis*, a series of three tests in reading, writing, and mathematics. Administered by the Educational Testing Service, which also oversees the SAT, the *Praxis* is billed as a reliable measure of prospective teachers' academic skills and required knowledge of their subject specialty. It has also proven to be a consistent barrier keeping Black teachers out of the profession. In June 2019, a work group of over 250 Baltimore teachers, other educators, and community members issued a report concluding that entrance exams that "affect Black teachers and teacher candidates inequitably" were one of several factors contributing to the decline of Black teachers in the city's schools.

Hall's test taking predated this finding, but her *Praxis* journey echoed the results of the group's paper. She passed the reading and writing sections on her second attempt, by cramming all the material from her undergraduate core English classes. After failing her first try by a few points, she rebounded. But not without tireless effort. "I made index cards labeled *The Harlem Renaissance* and *Dante's Inferno*, and put them on a little hook that I carried around, studying on my planning period at work," she sighed. "I had to [restudy] everything that I learned in college." Except Hall was no longer a student. She was a brand-new teacher responsible for five classes of students. A brand-new teacher who was required to pay fifty dollars out of pocket for each retest. A brand-new teacher who was stressed and worried and so discouraged that she almost gave up after missing the cutoff score for the math section of the licensing exam three times.

"I tried studying, but I didn't know how because I was never really very strong in math," she said. She bought practice books, took a prep course, and kept trying. In a stroke of serendipity, ETS introduced combination scores. On her fourth try she passed the math portion with a minimal score, and her combined score on all the sections guaranteed she would secure a teaching credential.

The prospect that LaQuisha Hall, Baltimore City Public Schools' 2018 Teacher of the Year, once came very close to throwing in the towel should sound an alarm for policymakers. Her journey to the classroom is representative of larger unanswered questions in education: How do we best prepare qualified teachers? How do we remove the obstacles to entry for Black teachers and other teachers of color? Should a single test solely determine a person's future in teaching? How do we make their first year the best year of many to come?

3

THE ROOKIE

The plot is a staple of inspirational teacher movies: a maverick rookie is assigned a class of impossible-to-teach students at an "inner-city" high school. Driven by an unexplained passion and an indefatigable work ethic, the rebel achieves a level of academic success never before seen with the students long ago written off. The implausible, yet feel-good, storyline of films like *Freedom Writers* and *Dangerous Minds* bears little relation to reality. For most new teachers, the beginning months in the classroom are a mix of trepidation, self-doubt, frustration, and angst. Whether a teaching novice successfully surfs the rough seas or wipes out has everything to do with planning, feedback, and support.

Hall was no exception. Walking into Edmondson-Westside High School in southwest Baltimore in September 2003, she had no say in the classes or grade levels she taught. These decisions fell to the principal and the administrative team. They needed an English teacher, and the twenty-one-year-old Hall filled the void. She was assigned two SAT prep and two creative writing classes for grades ten, eleven, and twelve, elective courses known at the time as "the dumping ground" for upperclassmen to meet their requirements. Initially, tasks like lesson planning and instruction were rote and tedious. "It took me a whole Saturday and Sunday and maybe part of a Friday to start my lesson plans for the following week, and maybe by the time Monday rolled around, I would only have three done; I was so stressed out," she recalls.

Even with a template, the lesson plan process required meticulous preparation—standards, student objectives, instructional strategies, intent. Neither of her classes had a curriculum, and she was going day-by-day in a workbook. The trickiest was the lesson duration; timing it precisely to the length of a class period. "As much time as I was putting in, I was still under-planning," she says. "They would've already finished all my work, and I'm scrambling with something for them to do." She adds with a laugh that sometimes her option of last resort was "Do it again."

By second semester she had picked up the class Black Literature—with an assigned textbook—and gained a more solid technique. She craved structure, and used the curriculum as a crutch to get familiar with what was required of her. "I followed that thing religiously," she says, "literally printing it out and highlighting the things that I had done. If it wasn't highlighted, that's where I would start the next day."

Consistency can feel safe for beginning teachers, like bumpers on a bowling lane. Eventually, with more experience comes the desire for the flexibility—and autonomy—to weave in unconventional methods to fill gaps in students' knowledge. But at first, Hall adopted the curriculum 100 percent, and relied heavily on the experience of her colleagues. A fellow teacher shared a syllabus that Hall tweaked, changing the name and modifying the class rules and procedures to match her own. Her approach to testing was also fairly standardized, with tests every Friday and heavily weighted exams at the end of each unit: "Early in my career, I felt the test was a requirement. Because I had been tested as a student, I would give tests like I remembered." Tests would later be shelved as she found more progressive, and more effective, ways to measure learning.

Clearly, Hall brought a range of assets to the classroom, like her creativity. She often received compliments from colleagues on the visual aspects of her bulletin board and lesson plans. She noticed it helped stimulate her students' creativity in class projects. But the learning curve was steep when it came to the administrative side of the job. The volume of paperwork, and the stress it places on teachers to find the time for non-instructional duties, is a complaint that always comes up in teacher survey results. She anticipated pulling out a lesson plan, teaching, and grading students' work. No one prepared her for navigating the parent emails, staff meetings, school committees, and field trip permission slips. It was the part of teaching Hall found most surprising as she went through her own stages of paperwork acceptance: resent, resist, adjust, and adapt.

Where she felt most at home was with students, even though she had limited experience with Black urban youth. As a Black teacher, not much older than the school's primarily Black student body, there was an easy rapport. At the outset she was the Southern belle, "nice to everybody, let's go to my house, you can have some pie." She quickly recognized the shortcomings of this tactic, as kids misread her niceness as feebleness. She took the "L" her first semester, observed some strict veteran teachers with orderly, quiet classrooms, and came back second semester a drill sergeant. "They were quiet, they listened, and I had the same outcome that I saw in the other classrooms," she says. "But what I didn't like was that they were so fearful of me."

Hall eventually discovered a balance between her Southernism and strictness, realizing she could maintain order without an iron fist. The significance of relationships in managing her classroom transformed her teaching. Classroom management is often presented as a prescriptive formula, with the teacher doling out rules to establish authority and minimize chaos. As a rookie, Hall uncovered what even many seasoned teachers overlook: everything that happens in the classroom is relational. With clear expectations, students make better decisions, reducing discipline issues. When inappropriate behavior does occur, relationships are the basis to reset and recover.

Discipline is an area where many new teachers are ill-equipped. Hall, who naturally had a way with young people, says too many newbies stumble due to inadequate teacher training. And she empathizes. "What if you've got a kid who is cussing you out and you've never been cussed out before . . . and you want to lash back out?" she asks. "They'll give you the one through five checklist of disciplinary action. Number one, warning. Number two . . . but what does that look like in real time?" In such a case, she recommends immediately removing that child from the class and having that conversation with them later. More important, leave room for forgiveness.

Early on she learned that forming relationships with kids

was an investment with incalculable dividends. Just as she was teaching them, they were educating her on how they needed to be taught. She easily connected with the girls in her classroom but struggled with the boys, having grown up without brothers. "I found myself being really hard on them," she says, because her expectations were so high for men in general. Over time she realized she was holding them responsible for behavioral skills they never developed. She adjusted, and tried to show and tell. It was an attitude shift that changed everything: "The way you teach them is by modeling it . . . [and] actually give them the opportunity to correct something that they may not have learned prior. Indirectly, they taught me not to be so hard on them."

Bonding with her students also led to some tough and humorous moments. Like teen girls oversharing. "They would have conversations with me in class like 'He wants to have sex and I'm not sure.' And I'm like, 'I'm not either, honey. I just want you to define those ten words on the board.'" In time, she would start an after-school mentoring program to provide the space for talking through such decisions, with parents' permission. In the moment, she had to maintain her professionalism and communicate that she heard them, but it was neither the time nor place.

Throughout the first year, Hall received critical support

from experienced teachers in Edmondson's English department. The department chair introduced her to the other English teachers and hinted that they should look out for her. But one teacher really took her under wing—answering all her questions, checking on her, loaning books, and packing lunch for the overworked beginner. With Regina Bullock, her "school mom," she brainstormed, wrote lesson plans, and organized joint classroom activities. Memories of the time they spent together over a decade ago leave her beaming with happiness.

As a twenty-one-year-old new to Baltimore, Hall was living on her own. Bullock made her feel anchored. "She didn't just help me with the pedagogy of a classroom, [but] the responsibility and leadership of being a positive representation for kids," she says admiringly. "Because of how giving she was to me, it caused me to be even more giving to my students . . . she was like the ultimate mentor."

Bullock even schooled Hall on the more mundane side of teaching in city schools, like paying teacher union dues. She had no idea what a union was, and was confused when her first pay stub had twenty-five dollars withdrawn for BTU. She went to Bullock, who explained the payroll deduction was for the Baltimore Teachers Union, to provide legal representation "if something goes wrong with your job" and to advocate on teachers' behalf. Still not convinced, Hall contemplated dropping her union membership and pocketing another fifty dollars a month, but she followed Bullock's advice and kept it. It was one of many ways her teacher mentor nudged her in the right direction.

Coaching new teachers was not a pattern for Bullock, who retired in 2010 after forty years of teaching English at Edmondson. But Hall stood out—she was studying at Morgan State, Bullock's alma mater; she was young; she had no family nearby; and the skilled teacher was drawn to her. In Hall, Bullock saw a confident greenhorn with promise and a special connection with young people. "She was no-nonsense, even though she was always a fun teacher," Bullock recalled. "The students loved her from the very beginning."

Yet Bullock emphasized the mutual benefits of mentoring, stressing that the give-and-take between her and Hall was invigorating, given she had been teaching more than thirty years. "I would go to LaQuisha's room because I think by that time I was on a downward turn as far as creativity was concerned," she says. "She had so many innovative ideas, colorful bulletin boards. She helped me in that way, and I provided stability for her." In the sixteen years since they met, the relationship has deepened. The women have shared Thanksgiving, Christmas, and Maryland crabs. Bullock remains a trusted influence, still guiding and motivating Hall to hang in there on her more challenging days.

The professional support that shaped Hall's rookie year, and permanently altered her teaching practice, is rare. More prevalent is the "sink or swim" mentality of throwing a new teacher into a classroom—diminishing the profession to a game of survival of the fittest. Exacerbating the situation is the solitary nature of teaching, with one adult working behind closed doors days on end. As cited in studies, isolation and lack of support remain a primary reason for new teachers exiting the profession, with novice teachers eventually succumbing to the stress and loneliness. But the status quo of slogging through until you figure it out is firmly baked into new teacher onboarding.

Heather Heffelmire, Hall's friend and colleague at Carver, can relate. Now in her fourth year, the spirited English teacher describes her debut in 2016 at another Baltimore high school: "I think of myself as a pretty resilient person. I was in the navy. I went to boot camp. And by my third or fourth day teaching, I was in my car crying because it was so hard." One pal she started with in September had quit by Halloween. The beginner leaned on another first-year teacher to commiserate and build up her morale.

Like Hall, Heffelmire came through a nontraditional

teaching program, Teach for America (TFA), and acknow-
ledges some people enter teaching when they are not suited
for it. "You bring people in who have no experience . . .
and it erupts," she warned. "It's a mess, and detrimental for
students." She has also seen great TFA teachers, however,
and points to structural barriers as an equal culprit. "We put
it on the individual, and I don't think that's fair," she insisted.
"Make sure that the right people are coming into the classroom, and make sure that when those right people come into
the classroom, they're given the necessary support to ensure
that they stay in the classroom."

Hall believes that forcing newbies to struggle is part
of the culture of teaching. She works to pay forward what
she received from Bullock, which has made her a force in
her school and district. On a summer Saturday afternoon,
she leads a workshop at a self-care day for Baltimore City
teachers, where she urges participants to counter isolation
by embracing collective care. In an exercise she dubs
"Balancing Your Balloons," Hall asks the audience to blow
up balloons, each one representing a test a new teacher
might encounter, such as drama with a parent, crafting a
lesson plan, or simply finding the time to eat lunch. She
then calls a volunteer to the front of the room and tosses
a balloon at her, one after the other—soon the teacher is

straining to juggle four to five balloons simultaneously, but no one jumps to assist.

"They watched, which is a common practice in education," Hall revealed. "We will see a teacher struggle, and we won't go to their aid." Why not? Some veterans prize being the best teacher in their building and might resist being outshined by newcomers; some consider struggling a rite of passage; some don't know how to help; others believe that help should come from the administration, aka "that's not in my pay grade." Regardless of the reason, it can leave new teachers feeling like a castaway on an island. Hall knows there's a better way to bring rookie teachers into the profession because she experienced it.

The following week her evangelizing continues when she addresses TFA corps members starting with Baltimore City Public Schools for the 2019 school year—a small act to guarantee the new class of Heather Heffelmires have a softer landing. Sharing the importance of reaching out, she tells the crowd to "ask as many questions as you want, harass as many people as you want, even when they get tired of you, the goal is that you improve." She also addresses the elephant in the room, specifically TFA's reputation for retaining teachers. TFA is the subject of frequent scorn within public education circles for fast-tracking individuals into teaching. But Hall has a pragmatic take centered, as is her custom, on kids.

"Support is important to me, not the program [the teacher comes through to arrive in the classroom]," she states. "Essentially, is there support backing this person who's walking into this new climate and atmosphere and gaining twenty to thirty faces that they've never seen before? I know when a teacher is new, and that's what I focus on." Her plea to senior teachers is to never forget what it felt like to be new, nervous, and unsure, and to extend a hand. Spoken with the confidence of an award-winning alternatively certified teacher.

"I wasn't just new, but I was super country," she quips. "I needed the opportunity to step my foot in the classroom . . . I loved it, and I found that I could do it well." With the help of an exceptional woman. "What a difference it made in my life and in my career . . . I definitely want to reciprocate all that she did for me to other new teachers."

4

REALITIES OF THE WORK

"I'm constantly fighting to help people see my profession is something to be valued, something to be admired . . . not ridiculed and criticized all the time." Hall's full-time mission is the nation's periodic agenda when Teacher Appreciation Week rolls around every May. Created in 1984 by the National PTA, it is a Hallmark-ish celebration observed by giving teachers gift cards, scented candles, homemade sweet treats, and tchotchkes emblazoned with apples, the proverbial symbol of knowledge and education. It is a week preceded and followed by fifty-one other weeks when the realities of teaching are more frazzled than festive.

Few professions are as fraught with assumptions and misunderstandings. Chief among them is the perception that teaching is an easy career track, one for people who lack ambition. The old adage "Those who can, do; those who can't, teach" still hangs like an albatross around the neck of the field's practitioners. Teachers often shoulder the burden of debunking stereotypes. Hall is not immune to this truth. She opened an Instagram account designed to promote the positives of Baltimore City teachers, students, and schools, and push back against the false and damaging narratives in the press and social media. "I am the most resistant teacher you will ever meet," she says, adding that there are people with opinions "who haven't stepped foot in our schools. I'm in the classroom. I'm there . . . so I have every right to tell you why you're wrong."

She thinks much of the perception comes from the fact that teachers spend their days with kids. A job in which children are the client is easy to dismiss, allowing people to forget that teaching requires education and skill and training. It is also a job with a high degree of responsibility. Teachers are entrusted with the development of someone else's child. Hall believes people are much harder on teachers because they work with children. The irony, though, is that the nature of teaching means those in the profession need less public flogging—and more support—to improve.

The stigma is even more acute in high-poverty districts like Baltimore. Substitutes and inexperienced teachers are more prevalent in under-resourced schools like Carver. She theorizes that these two things are connected, with the negativity forcing some teachers to question "investing all this time and money just for people to say [unkind] things" about her vocation. But Hall is undeterred, and devoted to enriching young Black minds in the city's schools. She briefly flirted with the idea of moving to a school in suburban Baltimore County, near her home, but feels a kinship with Baltimore youth. "I feel I can offer them something," she says. "I know there are students in the county that could benefit from what I have to offer, but county students already have a lot."

Brendan Penn, a STEM teacher at Lyons Mill Elementary in Owings Mills, Maryland, agrees. Although working in a suburban district brings its own advantages and drawbacks, he says, such as contending with the misnomer "suburban." Far from a quaint hamlet near the city, Baltimore County is the twenty-fifth largest school district in the country, with 115,000 students and 175 schools. "There are pockets of inequity that can exist, serving such a large population and vast number of schools," says Penn, who was named Baltimore County Teacher of the Year the same year Hall was recognized. On the upside, he said, working in a district with strong community support means his students benefit from financial resources "to support your vision, your classroom, and your school." Baltimore

County is also a district that is whiter and more affluent than the city that shares its name.

Irrespective of a district's size, wealth, or demographics, certain challenging realities of teaching are universal. Working with parents is a prerequisite that can be both daunting and rewarding. When Hall's freshman class self-published a book, family members flocked to her classroom for the signing ceremony. They were enamored with Hall, and it showed. "Some students in my classes hated reading before the year started, and their parent was sitting in the audience watching them be acknowledged for being a published author," she says. "That meant a lot to the kids and the families that came." But not every teacher-parent interaction is as upbeat.

Conversations about a child who is flunking or has fallen behind can be tense. She knows parents have good intentions and want the best for their child—so do teachers. The tricky part is when parents want an immediate fix to the problem. "I need parents to understand that when teachers tell them their child is failing, that doesn't mean your child is a failure. It means that they need some more support," she counsels. "Teachers and parents butt heads because we think [support] needs to be an ongoing practice with your child . . . helping them with the skills. With parents, it's

what can my child do today to get where they need to be."
Similarly frustrating are calls home about student miscon-
duct, which she quickly realized annoyed the kids and the
parents, and rarely corrected the misbehavior.

Hall eventually adopted a rose-colored glasses approach
to parent outreach. She resolves student conflicts in the classroom. She holds her students accountable for their academic
progress. And she only contacts parents with good news—
reversing the pattern of teachers calling home when a child
has done something wrong. When it comes to this aspect of
the job, she sees parents at PTA nights, invites them into the
classroom, and steers them to her Instagram account.

Another discovery for Hall was that all teaching is political. As a teacher, she is a public employee—public schools
are operated by districts under the authority of state
governments, putting teachers in the same category as public
servants like firefighters and sanitation workers. What sets
teaching apart is the political scrutiny: federal legislation
emphasizing teacher accountability; state legislation tinker-
ing with curriculum, testing, and teacher evaluation systems;
and politicians wielding excessive influence over what—and
how—children are taught in America's classrooms.

Dodo Seriki, the Morgan State University educator, says
the degree to which politics impact education is the biggest

eye-opener for new teachers. Undergraduate teacher education spends little time talking about the politics that will shape their work in the classroom, she says, leaving them gobsmacked once they enter public schools and grasp how the decisions of school boards and state governments affect resources in their building. For Hall, one of the most pernicious effects of policymakers' sway is the governmental mandate to raise standardized test scores. She purposely requests English 1 every year because freshmen are not state tested.

"I don't want to be part of any of that," she protests. "They're already up against the greatest tests that people can experience, which is surviving in a city that is out to kill them every single day, or make them look bad. If they can come to school every day, I don't feel like we should give them another test . . . they passed."

Sidney Thomas, a teacher friend at Baltimore's Holabird Academy, echoes Hall's frustration. The educator recalled testing days that "sucked the life out of everybody," and to make it worse, teachers received the data too late for it to be useful. "Students take the test in May. You get the data back in October. I teach eighth grade, and they're not even at my school anymore," she explains. "You're not getting the results back when you're teaching them. So how does that help me?"

Missing from the glossy career brochure was any mention of the nights and weekends spent grading, summers racking up professional development credits, and the emotional and intellectual toils of the job. After years of an aching back from carrying student folders and books home every night, Hall decided to ditch the routine her fourth year of teaching. She remarks casually that she now uses her workday efficiently, capitalizing on planning periods to grade.

But there's a tradeoff: Hall also adds an hour to her workday to avoid taking other schoolwork home. While she's not lugging a heavy bag anymore, the work can still follow her home, whether it is brainstorming lesson ideas or role-playing thorny situations. "Taking work home doesn't always equate to grading papers. You can be thinking about that kid that you know needs more, and you haven't figured out the way to give him more yet," she says. It is also not unusual for a steady stream of Instagram notifications from students to light up her phone after school. She knows all their handles, and responds with a compliment or encouraging message.

Juggling work and home is a balancing act. Through the good days and bad, her husband, Mardis, is a sounding board, helping her sort out her thinking over a home-cooked meal. As part of their marital bargain, the internet entrepreneur does the cooking. They married in 2005, when she had only been teaching a couple of years, and he has had a front-row seat on her journey—the learning curve, the success stories, and the mishaps. "She really embraces the work that she does," he says, noting that after so many years, and having taught thousands of students, the spillover to home is unavoidable. "For the most part, I serve on the perimeter," he says. "Listening to what went well, what went crazy . . . irate parents and congratulatory moments." Mardis fills LaQuisha's unscheduled time with movie nights and ice cream dates to decompress—knowing that free time in teaching can be elusive, and the hype about working bankers' hours and enjoying summers off is an enduring myth.

Related is the legend of the overpaid teacher. Analysts at the left-leaning Economic Policy Institute report that teachers were paid 21.4 percent less in weekly wages than similar college-educated workers in 2018—and in terms of total compensation (wages plus benefits) teachers earned 13.1 percent less than college graduates in comparable fields. With a median annual salary of just under $58,000, teachers are paid some three thousand dollars below the median salary of other college graduates with a bachelor's degree, and almost fifteen thousand dollars below the median salary of those with a master's degree—all the more salient as 58 percent of teachers have a master's or higher degree.

When school is not in session, public educators often take summer jobs, teach summer school, or take professional development courses—occasionally on their own dime. Hall did all of it at various stages of her career, as have her teaching colleagues. Penn has worked every summer since he started in Baltimore County eight years ago. Traditionally, teachers receive a paycheck over a ten-month period (i.e., September through June) making budgeting more difficult in the two months without a regular income. Penn's second jobs—camp counselor, tutor, and robotics coach—have all centered on education. His teaching acquaintances are somewhat less mission-driven, choosing to bartend, waitress, and babysit to offset the lack of pay during the summer break. Some school districts offer teachers the option of spreading their salary out over twelve months; the downside being a smaller monthly paycheck.

Thomas also tutored and did curriculum writing when she first started teaching. Now married with a two-income household, working over the summer to make ends meet is less pressing. It is a scenario she acknowledged is the exception, not the norm. Roughly 16 percent of teachers, or one in six, will spend their summers supplementing their salary, driving for rideshare companies or moonlighting at fast-food restaurants, according to a Pew Research Center analysis. Younger and newer teachers are more likely to hold a summer job. About the same number (18 percent) had jobs during the school year, but there was no variation in age or experience for those teachers earning extra income.

Hall started with a salary in the mid-$30Ks that she found sufficient, though notably she was living paycheck to paycheck. "I was able to survive. I wasn't eating shrimp and lobster, but I wasn't scrambling for food either," she says. With her master's degree came a salary increase, with incremental raises for longevity over the course of her career. Winning Teacher of the Year in 2018 boosted her salary, putting her comfortably above the high-$60Ks.

Teacher salaries fluctuate widely between states, as does the cost of living across regions. The average salary for public school teachers in 2017–18 was $60,483, per federal education data. Hall's state of Maryland ranked seventh in teacher pay, coming in at $69,761. Among the highest-paying states are New York ($83,585), California ($81,126), Massachusetts ($79,710), and Connecticut ($73,113). Among the lowest-ranked states for teacher pay are Arizona ($47,746), Florida ($47,721), Oklahoma ($45,678), and West Virginia ($45,642).

With educated professionals relentlessly pursuing side

hustles, the issue of teacher pay came to a head in 2018, climaxing in statewide strikes and walkouts by teachers across the nation. Educators in West Virginia started the revolt with a nine-day strike in February that won them an average 5 percent pay raise. Soon other states joined the effort, with teachers in Arizona, Oklahoma, and Kentucky protesting inadequate pay and school funding. The subject of pay elicits broad discontent, as stated by Phi Delta Kappa in its 2019 Poll of the Public's Attitudes Toward the Public Schools. In the survey, 55 percent of teachers would vote to strike for higher pay—and parents and the public firmly have teachers' backs: 74 percent of parents and 71 percent of all adults would support teachers in their community striking for a pay increase.

Nationwide, strikes extending into 2019 sent a strong message about the dismal state of teacher salaries. Many teachers admitted to feeling stretched past their limits, underpaid and unreimbursed for classroom supplies and materials spent on their students. According to a National Center for Education Statistics survey released in May 2018, 94 percent of public school teachers spent an average of $479 to stock their classrooms with notebooks, crayons, folders, pencils, and much more in the 2014–15 school year. Whereas Hall has never shirked from spending her own money on her scholars, teacher out-of-pocket spending is a contentious topic. Even within her professional circle, the views on the practice differ.

Some years Hall has spent close to one thousand dollars on books, room décor, and other extras to make her classroom more inviting. She views it as a worthwhile investment, having seen how classroom aesthetics can influence learning. "When you put some effort into the room, kids put some effort into your class," she states. "I've seen how having a visually appealing classroom can transform what you get from the students." On Twitter she was more blunt about the expense of decorating her room, writing that "my scholars walk outside and see too many [ramshackle] houses . . . they don't go on vacations, and all they know and see is Baltimore. My goal is to give them the best school experience."

Penn is similarly unapologetic about spending on his Baltimore County kids. Teaching elementary-level STEM, he spends between three hundred to five hundred dollars of his own money a year to supplement science and tech projects. He also reaps the benefits of teaching in a suburban school where fundraisers for classroom activities are ingrained in the culture. By contrast, in southeast Baltimore, Thomas spent two hundred dollars one year setting up her class library—going to yard sales and Goodwill to buy books. The constant outlay of personal cash on school supplies felt unsustainable with a child of her own. "I disagree with the fact that we as teachers have to spend money out of pocket, or ask for some type of handout, to get simple things like novels . . . all of my money can't keep getting funneled into the classroom," she says.

Thomas hints at a sentiment captured in the PDK Poll that tied school underfunding to the psychology of teachers feeling undervalued. As they advocate for more money for schools, some educators are taking it upon themselves to lift morale through supportive in-school networks. Like a sunflower reaching for the sun, Hall spotted that her colleagues grew taller when recognized by their peers. Her response was a year-long campaign called "Happy Mail" where Carver faculty anonymously exchange small gifts and notes throughout the year to build camaraderie and teamwork. Akin to "Secret Santa," teachers share their favorite color, snack, and restaurant—and in turn, another staff member secretly leaves a matching present in their school mailbox each month.

The power of being seen and appreciated can be underrated. The big reveal of each person meeting their gift-giver is a jubilant display of excitement and intimacy. Sitting in a circle, the voices of the staff crescendo, beginning to sound like a room of youngsters talking over each other. Reminiscing over the personally tailored gifts—coloring books, Halos oranges, journals, and pistachios—Carver's educators express the delight that comes from catching a rewarding moment in a sea of challenges. Hall's objective—to uplift the teachers in her building by practicing mutual care—is achieved.

5

STAYING POWER

With Hall's rookie year behind her, the summer should have been a time to relax, refresh, and enjoy a well-deserved break. But she was too stressed to feel blessed. Her mind was preoccupied with the new school year two months away. Her anxiety rose as questions circled in her head: *Should I have documented what worked last year? Will I forget everything over the summer? Do I need to start writing lesson plans?* In her early years of teaching, so much felt familiar yet frightening. No longer brand new, she understood the basics, but was still green enough that doubt was part of the job.

Hall settled into the cycles of the school year. It was like running a marathon. Out of the gate strong in September, she was enthusiastic and excited, even as she coped with the angst that came from an incoming class. By October, she would hit her stride. By the holiday season in November and December, she was losing steam. But the dawn of a new semester in January signaled a fresh start, reviving her for the months ahead. The vibe from her scholars kept her afloat during the long stretch until spring break. Rounding the turn into the final straightaway, she could push through to June, breaking the ribbon at the finish line of another academic year.

What sustained her those initial years at Edmondson-Westside was the community of teachers who embraced her. Nicknaming her "Baby Girl," anytime she was frustrated, they ushered her into an office where veteran teachers pulled out the manual, flipped through the pages, and found a solution. "There were times that I thought I didn't want to do it anymore, because of the stress in the moment," she says, crediting the teaching team with helping her recalibrate on nerve-racking days. As time passed, she felt less like a novice, figuring she had made mistakes, recovered, and learned—be it classroom management or curriculum.

Toward the end of her second year she "started to be looked at as a leader versus someone who needed help," she says. Hall caught the eye of her superiors for creating a culture that extracted the best from students. It was a climate grounded in relationship-building and trust between a Black teacher and her scholars. She was tapped to help incoming teachers at Edmondson, doling out advice and sharing her best practices. Word spread about the young innovator at Edmondson. During her fifth year, she was recruited to lead the English department at Forest Park High School in northwest Baltimore.

Leaving behind her safety net, the twenty-five-year-old took the helm of Forest Park's largest department, which included twelve English teachers. The reception was frosty. Hall was younger and newer to teaching than her direct reports, resulting in bouts of resentment. To weather the friction, she applied motivational tricks acquired in the classroom, and watched relations thaw. Tensions waned after she instituted Teacher of the Month, hanging their pictures up in the office and distributing goody bags filled with teacher supplies. "They saw that I was on their side," she says.

The good times were short-lived. At the close of the school year, Forest Park was reconstituted, and the entire staff was replaced—from the principal to the custodians. Each former employee had to reapply for their jobs. School reconstitution is a dramatic policy solution for turning around chronically underperforming schools. The theory is that "persistently failing" schools demand radical, rather than incremental, change. Evidence suggests the opposite.

In a paper published by WestEd, a national nonprofit education agency, researcher Jennifer O'Day concluded that changing a school requires vision and a long-range plan, and long-term gains in student performance "don't automatically follow from a personnel sweep."

The strategy also fails to account for unintended consequences, like the loss of experienced educators. At Forest Park, the principal who had hired Hall was gone, and the replacement was a young white principal who determined that Hall was "kind of young" to be a department head. Turned off by his comment, she left Forest Park after a year.

A wealth of support and experiencing "so much success in that short amount of time" sustained her during her early years: "I was already helping my department head at Edmondson, and I transitioned to a department head myself in my first five years." That phase of her career also solidified a desire to be in the classroom. Bucking the trend of experienced teachers exiting for administrative positions, she enthusiastically returned to full-time teaching. "I want to stay where there's a need," she states, "and I know there's a need for teachers in Baltimore City."

For decades, researchers have reported that an estimated 40 to 50 percent of new teachers leave the profession within five years of entry. With more accurate, national longitudinal data, University of Pennsylvania education professor Richard Ingersoll, an expert on teacher attrition, figures that 44.6 percent of new teachers in public (and private) schools leave within five years, and well over one-third (39 percent) within four years. Ingersoll and his co-authors, in an October 2018 report, also uncovered interesting nuances in the data: among women-dominated fields, teachers quit more frequently than nurses (30 percent to 19 percent); and among similar intellectually demanding jobs, teacher quit rates exceeded lawyers (19 percent) and engineers (16 percent.)

Teacher resignations were highest in urban, high-poverty, and rural public schools, and in schools with large concentrations of nonwhite students—nearly half of all public school teacher turnover takes place in just one quarter of the total number of U.S. public schools. Teachers of color left the profession at significantly higher rates than white teachers. The findings dovetail with Hall's observations on the teacher workforce. Over the span of seventeen years, at seven Baltimore schools, she has only worked at one site—Edmondson—where the English teaching staff continued year to year. As the school year ended, at least three teachers from Carver's English department planned not to return in September, choosing to transfer to another school or leave the profession altogether. Frankly, Hall questioned whether they would last until June. "New teachers at my school stay two to three years in my department," she notes.

The lack of stability at Carver is more than a staffing problem. The constant churn negatively impacts her students' progress—without a regular teacher to fill the slot, some classes are led by a rotation of substitutes the entire school year. The overreliance on temporary instructors undermines student learning and morale. Solving the revolving door—what some experts have termed "a leaky bucket"—is vital for her Black students to stay on pace. "Part of the reason why our kids are so behind is because of the turnover. You go a year without a math class. And then they put you in the next level of math the following year. Now you're really struggling."

The adverse effects of leaving her students without a teacher is the number one reason Heffelmire, Hall's colleague, stays. With four years of experience, she knows the rarity of teachers making it past the five-year mark. Chronic teacher shortages in majority-Black schools means "our students are not being served. They are not being taught," she says. Rather than a coincidence, she sees the perpetual underfunding of schools like hers as a reflection of the larger societal disregard for Black communities.

Awakened by the Black Lives Matter movement, she considers Carver the place where she can initiate the greatest change. "I go into the classroom with the mindset: 'How can I give my students the skills and the knowledge to critique society, and then feel empowered enough to do something about it?'"

She is also strengthened by the abundance of guidance she receives from Hall, whom she fondly refers to as "teacher goals." Heffelmire pops by room 263, surveying the bookshelves and chatting about new YA releases. Following in Hall's footsteps, she opened a class Instagram account and started calling her kids scholars. Still in the novice stage, her longevity is due in part to having the humility to ask for help. "Sometimes, as teachers, there's this weird competitiveness that can be fueled in schools," she explains. "Really knowing I have a lot to learn, and I have a lot of great teachers I can learn from" boosts her as she nears the five-year milestone.

Teachers helping teachers is a supplement, not a replacement, for the systemic support that early-career teachers require. One proven remedy for turnover is districts providing mentoring programs and ongoing training for newcomers. The New Teacher Center, a California-based nonprofit focused on teacher effectiveness, also underscores the role of school principals, citing that "inadequate support from school administration is one of the three most often reported causes of a new teacher's decision to leave the profession."

Once relegated to the role of building managers, successful principals today must serve multiple functions: instructional coach, head cheerleader, consensus builder, and visionary leader. Fashioning a positive school climate is directly linked to teachers' spirits and job satisfaction.

The nonprofit group recommended a range of tactics for retaining teachers, advising principals to introduce new teachers to their colleagues, hold regular meetings with new teachers to build trust and allow for necessary questions, and keep the most challenging students from being disproportionately placed in beginning teachers' classrooms. The heavy administrative workload of principals can lead them to overlook rudimentary steps when onboarding new teachers. This assumes new recruits are a good fit for the school—not always a safe assumption, says Euna McGruder, a twenty-year veteran school administrator.

Her method to improve retention puts greater scrutiny on teacher hiring, which she implemented as principal at Baltimore's Booker T. Washington Middle School. At the time, it was among the lowest-performing schools in Maryland, with a high level of principal and teacher turnover.

McGruder was the eleventh principal in three years, and the majority of the teaching staff was new.

She sought candidates who would understand, respect, and mesh with her school's learners, instead of someone with just a stellar GPA. The attributes to teach students in a school listed as "persistently dangerous" by the federal government "is completely different from hiring in Orange County, California," she says, spoken with the expertise of a Black woman who has led schools in four states. "I want you in front of my children for five minutes so that I can see the engagement," she continues, emphasizing the importance of a prospective hire's cultural competency.

In this regard, Hall stood out. By McGruder's assessment, she had the combination of skill and will to thrive in urban education. Yet by her own admission, Hall still had aspects to learn. Like realizing that teachers received personal days. She had no idea that she could take a day off her first three years, aiming for perfect attendance as a carryover from her days as a student.

It was the knack for connecting with Black kids that was her most formative attribute. Reports from colleagues showed the efficacy of her approach. Whereas children were resistant and defiant with them, with Hall the same kids were responsive and diligent. She decided it was because she rejected the stereotype of the "problem-ridden Black inner-city teen."

Forming real bonds with students meant she could identify when a child was tired from hunger or facing a hardship, as opposed to laying his head on the desk because he stayed up all night on his cell phone. Outsiders assume, because the students are Black and living in Baltimore, that some larger social condition is at fault. She knows better. "A lot of times my kids from two-parent homes stay up playing video games. They're tired because they caused themselves to be tired," she relates. "We do have students that go through a lot, but all of our kids are not struggling in the way that people perceive them to be."

Some struggles are universal. She noticed the same group of teenage girls would gather in her room to talk when school ended, some of whom were not even her students. It was the impetus for Hall starting a mentoring program for young girls. "I didn't have a good relationship with my mom. So many things that I wanted to talk to her about didn't feel comfortable," she reveals. "I wanted to create a safe place for them to talk to women about whatever they were experiencing." Conceived in 2006 during her time at Edmondson and formally launched in 2008, Queendom T.E.A. (Talented, Educated, Authentic) is an after-school club where conversations run the gamut from menstrual cycles to annoying parents to the street violence in Baltimore. More than one thousand girls have participated in Queendom over the last decade, and in 2019 its first scholarship of five hundred dollars was awarded to a Carver senior attending St. Mary's College.

Throughout her career, the program has followed Hall with each transition to a new school. A lasting remnant of her earliest days in the classroom. "There's a big conversation in education about building relationships. Teachers can't do that talking to kids about the syllabus," she urges. "You don't have a relationship because a kid sat in your classroom completing assignments. That's just a kid fulfilling the student role."

6

MASTERING THE CRAFT

" I know I'm doing well when kids are active in my class." The insight was part of Hall's journey in mastering the fundamentals of teaching—culminating in fostering a classroom community that takes risks and resists conformity. Around the five-year mark, with roughly ten thousand classroom hours, Hall felt proficient, competent, and confident in her teaching. Eventually the distinctions that indicate a sense of mastery—identifying student success, evaluating effectiveness, and making adjustments—began to emerge and intensify.

Rather than taking it personally when kids gave her a blank stare or an elongated sigh, Hall decided she had to work a little harder on getting their buy-in. Her routine of revising lesson plans to make the same books more fun was met with students' groans and complaints. A universal tenet of teaching is the need to be flexible and responsive, experimenting to match the needs and strengths of all learners. Quick thinking is an irreplaceable skill in the classroom. Hall adapted and thought creatively about what would make kids come alive. Strictly adhering to the curriculum seemed less important than finding ways to ignite their intellectual curiosity.

Noted poet and children's author Lucille Clifton, a National Book Award winner and the first Black woman to be awarded the Poetry Foundation's prestigious Ruth Lilly Poetry Prize, famously stated, "The literature of America should reflect the children of America." Hall thought about this plenty as she progressed in her career—a circuitous route from Forest Park in 2007, to teaching English in three different Baltimore middle schools and the district's alternative school for disciplined students, and then to Carver in 2015. Curriculum mandates passed down from the district's headquarters contradicted her experiences with so-called rigorous texts that her scholars summarily rejected. The information vacuum led to decisions about the English curriculum that felt arbitrary and misinformed.

For years Hall toed the line, abiding by scripted teaching as expected. Until the self-professed rule follower decided to deviate—incorporating a more inclusive set of authors and ditching the entire class reading and analyzing the same book that is commonplace in high school English. The plan carried risks. It was not unusual for the principal or other school leaders to drop by unannounced to observe her class. Her actions were subversive and liberating.

She introduced the assigned curriculum text to students by reading an excerpt from the first chapter. Then she exposed students to its structure and themes, using the book to teach that quarter's skill, such as completing an argumentative essay or a character analysis. For students interested in the mandated text, they continued reading it. Roughly 90 percent of a class would choose to opt out of the required reading for a book of their choice. That majority would be tasked with critically analyzing their book's themes, characters, setting, and historical context—and demonstrating the quarterly skill using one of the dozens of racially and culturally diverse books in her expansive class library.

The gamble paid off. Last year an administrator popped into English 1, where scholars should have been reading Lorraine Hansberry's groundbreaking 1959 play *A Raisin in the Sun*. The class read the first act together, and a few wanted to know what happened next. The rest of the room grumbled about reading a play. The dissenters split into multiple groups of four, each group choosing their own books. The small-group environment allowed students to work with and learn from their peers, holding lively discussions in literature circles about their selections. The visitor arrived, asking the kids what they were learning from reading Lorraine Hansberry's classic. "Oh, it's just like Baltimore," a youngster responded. "It's about a family and they were trying to be successful and stuff kept getting in their way." After delivering their unvarnished and astute response, the child returned to reading their non-sanctioned book. The administrator was unfazed.

It wasn't until she had matured in her career that Hall embraced student voice and choice. Previously, she let her scholars' perspectives and beliefs guide her teaching; now she was letting them choose the books they wanted to read. Her approach is based on closely watching their behaviors. Everyone reading the identical book allows kids to fade into the background, because someone else can answer the questions, she states. "When you have to talk about your book, you have to pay attention."

Hall's method is costing her time and dollars. She reads the YA books on her shelves before her scholars do so she can converse with them, teach the concepts they need to learn, and "help them better articulate their points." Before the 2018 school year ended, she had already acquired and started reading the 2019–20 book list picks from Project LIT, a national grassroots literacy network of teachers and students. The titles included *Anger Is a Gift*, which features a sixteen-year-old gay Black protagonist; *Internment*, a dystopian and chillingly plausible novel about the forced confinement of Muslim Americans; and *Monster*, the tale of a Black teen caught in the criminal justice system.

"I have so many to read because I'm doing it my way," she says, knowing that independence means continually finding donors to support her book-buying habit, which costs in the range of five hundred to six hundred dollars a year. Supplementing the curriculum is pricey. A room full of scholars reading books that mirror their lives and stimulate their thinking is priceless, she says, ensuring they feel seen and valued in literature. Many of her boys had failed English and came to her as freshmen convinced they didn't like to read. Now they complete an average of eight to nine books a year in English 1. Her triumphs are noteworthy for a group of kids who "only read the books required of them in school before, and never read on their own."

As some colleagues gripe that only a handful of kids are in their seats when the bell rings, Hall says youngsters *want* to be in her English class, boasting of near-full participation in every period. Along with strong student engagement, the degree of uniqueness that she can bring to her lessons is how she judges her success. Authors of culturally conscious

YA books that her students are reading make stops in her classroom. "The kids are more receptive to teachers who aren't sticking to worksheets," she says, describing projects that left her scholars stunned at how much they learned without a notebook or any paper. Teacher authority is often characterized as wielding a firm and controlling hand over students. Far from it. It takes a formidable teacher to listen to and hear students, and value their input on how they want to be taught.

Some days the most challenging aspect of the job is not the teaching, but the other adults in her building. Fighting the temptation to become jaded and complacent takes effort. Hall sees fellow veterans discouraged and dissatisfied from the weight of personal and professional pressures. Every workplace has energy vampires—people who zap your emotional strength with negative chatter. Hall finds the pessimism draining, since it's hard to encourage her kids if she's not feeling encouraged. She is sympathetic to her peers, but unmoved: "Everything I put my hands on I want to shine, so if you're talking poorly about my place of work, I'm going to let you know I'm there. There is some shine to this. That's my stance."

Staying upbeat is an intentional way of being. It is a requirement for staying innovative. She spends a significant amount of her time researching how to be a better educator. "I don't wait for them to come out with a new curriculum, because I don't feel we should wait on somebody else to dictate the trajectory of our jobs," she says. In mid-June, Hall's strategy for the following year is already taking shape. Unopened boxes of new books are tucked into empty corners, waiting to be read. She excitedly brainstorms what she wants to teach in September. Years of experience soothes the anxiety she once felt about the impending school year.

Preparation and self-education underlie all good teaching. It is a cycle of forward thinking that never really stops. When the district's reading curriculum assigned *Persepolis*, an autobiographical graphic novel that recounts author Marjane Satrapi's childhood in Iran, Hall knew little about the region, its history, and the country's Islamic Revolution. She read extensively in order to have deeply informed conversations with students. "A lot of times educators have to educate themselves," she maintains. "It's an expectation as a practitioner . . . you have to be a student first yourself."

The rapid spread of social media has made information widely available and democratized the profession—allowing teachers to form communities. Social media is invaluable to Hall's professional growth, whether building on what she already knows or attaining new skills via hashtags geared toward English language arts teachers. For National Poetry Month in April, she borrowed an idea posted on the Instagram account of the National Council of Teachers of English (NCTE) to help her scholars analyze Maya Angelou's "Phenomenal Woman" and Sojourner Truth's "Ain't I a Woman?" speech. Creating colorful illustrations and hand-lettered quotes gave students an artistic reprieve from another writing assignment.

Through the randomness of social networking, Hall learned about NCTE's Instagram post from another teacher's Twitter. "I wish I could've had that online education community when I first came into teaching," says Hall, who started in 2003. Twitter launched in 2006; Instagram in 2010. "It's a reciprocation of creative ideas, which I appreciate because I hate using the copy machine."

Besides novelty, she aims for impact in her lessons, prioritizing content that helps her scholars make connections to what's happening outside of the classroom. As she grew more confident in her teaching, she realized that topics drawn from real-life situations resonated most with kids. Outside speakers, such as Baltimore author D. Watkins, who writes about the city's racial struggles and inequities, became a fixture in her class "because if it's not relevant to them, they don't know why they're learning it." Leaving room for fun is equally important. A March Madness reading competition featured Hall tossing a basketball across the room; whoever caught it had to present their book to the class.

"Those are the things that make them want to come back to class the next day," she insists. "I had a student write on Instagram that my class was the best class he ever had. I think he said that because I wasn't inside a box with how I approach teaching. And they didn't have to be inside a box in how they learned."

For decades, scholars have validated Hall's unconventional ways by documenting the positive effects of culturally sustaining educators. Noted education professor Gloria Ladson-Billings in 1994 published *The Dreamkeepers: Successful Teachers of African American Children*, a pioneering look at the teaching methods that proved most successful with Black children. The acclaimed book profiled eight teachers whose "intellectually rigorous" classrooms showcased student-centered teaching that affirmed and strengthened children's cultural identity—the genesis of what we now know as culturally responsive, anti-racist pedagogy. A peer-reviewed article in the journal *Educational Psychologist* further explored this concept in 2018.

In "Black and Belonging at School," researchers concluded that Black students exposed to culturally affirming teaching have opportunities "to explore their racial identities in a context that legitimizes their culture, thereby allowing them to see commonalities and take pride in connections to people who look like them." Even with multiple studies, though, this kind of teaching is not always endorsed. In a widely reported lawsuit from 2016, English teacher Jeena Lee-Walker claimed she was fired from a New York City high school for a lesson on the wrongfully convicted Central Park Five after administrators allegedly told her the topic would "rile up" Black students.

For a time, Hall was fearful of being reprimanded for her teaching style, and wary of supervisors entering her classroom. She's not afraid anymore. "I'm doing what's best for kids," she says, no longer concerned about the repercussions. Fortunately, support for teaching practices that incorporate students' cultural backgrounds appears to be growing. A fifty-state analysis conducted in 2019 by the New America Foundation found that every state had integrated some facets of culturally responsive pedagogy into their teaching standards, although the descriptions from state to state were ambiguous.

Education is consumed with buzzwords—from the whole child model and social-emotional learning, which focuses on a holistic approach to students' health and well-being, to inquiry-based instruction, which is driven by student questioning and problem-solving. There is no single teaching approach that works best with every student. Yet Hall believes there are conditions in which Black urban students thrive, especially when content connects to their day-to-day reality and teachers connect to them as learners. In room 263, anything that fails to seize the attention of her scholars is promptly discarded and replaced. "I break the scripted curriculum tradition to ensure that the future of my students has some cushion to it . . . we talk so much about academia and there's not enough to prepare them for what's waiting for them on the other side, outside of academia."

As her inclusive teaching practices intensified, her viewpoint on testing shifted. She noticed that before a test, most of her kids were worried and nervous. She determined that students who did well were better test takers, and some kids performed poorly but still knew the material. The qualitative data was convincing. About five years ago she completely cut routine tests out of her class. She now gives a midterm and a final, both required in Baltimore City Schools. At the beginning of the year she also conducts an exam to benchmark their reading and comprehension levels.

What Hall is trying to foster in her classroom is the value of learning for its own sake, by diminishing the emphasis on test results and boosting reading as its own reward. "I'm always talking to them about their book, listening to their group conversations, and asking them questions to see what they know. I test them every day," she says.

On Fridays she summarizes that week's classwork: Monday's Socratic seminar, Tuesday's book café, Wednesday's picture depicting their main character's traits, and so forth. Each child's two weekly grades are derived from participation—how much reading was completed—and the individual assignment they want scored. Her technique reflects students' differentiated strengths, and accommodates varied learning preferences, including auditory, visual, and kinesthetic (hands-on, tactile activities).

Stressing that students are individuals, and should be treated as such, Hall spurns whole-class assignments. "If you're not a strong writer, but you're a great artist . . . why can't you turn that in instead?" she asks. The week's assignment is always accompanied by a reflection in which her scholars share their trouble spots, and tell Hall why they selected that piece of work to be graded. She argues that no student should fail her class because they need more help or a different teaching approach. "You shouldn't fail because you didn't know it! Maybe I failed in teaching it to you in the way that you needed, so now my job is to reteach it."

Her thinking seems revolutionary given the ingrained pass/fail culture in schools. It also runs contrary to today's testing craze. Hall challenges the view that only knowledge that is tested is valid. "The purpose in you coming to my class is not to get a number," she says. "It is to get an education." She proudly relates that less than ten kids out of 120-odd students in four classes failed in the 2018 school year, and the majority of failing marks went to no-show students.

As with student assessment, mastering the fundamentals of teaching has meant following her intuition and improvising. Great educators bring themselves into the classroom, and their teaching is infused with their interests, values, wittiness, and quirks. At its core, teaching is an extraordinarily human career. In the case of unmotivated students, Hall is quick-witted and nimble-minded. At times, when a child wasn't dazzled by her lesson, it would kill her vibe. "I could be doing jumping jacks with fire coming through my mouth . . . and some kids would still prefer not to come," she teases. Gradually she sensed that the way to overcome the apathy was putting students in charge of their learning.

"When kids tell me they don't like reading, I tell them you just haven't found the right book," she says. "If you are mathematical, you might like science books. You might not like a story of a Black boy growing up in Baltimore. Coming from middle school, reading *Diary of a Wimpy Kid*, you can transition into graphic novels. There are books out there for everybody; they have to find the one they like."

Reaching this level of mastery over seventeen years encompasses more than teaching content—there are other aspects to her expertise. Her large personality is a secret weapon, winning kids over with self-deprecating humor and easy banter. Her humility and compassion allows students to take risks and learn from their mistakes. Her discipline is defined by its Latin root, *discere*, meaning "to learn." Sitting in a coffee shop ticking off career insights, there was an overriding takeaway. "Holding kids responsible is not just punishment. Teachers will say 'I'm teaching them the real world.' But in the real world, if you're late with a bill payment, sometimes they'll waive the late fee. I want to teach them the real world, too. By showing mercy and grace."

7

BECOMING A LEADER

That morning dawned like every other. On school-days, Hall wakes up before the birds to pray, read, and prepare her mind and spirit for the workday. Except April 25, 2018, was unlike most Wednesdays. News reports indicated that Baltimore City Schools would be announcing its Teacher of the Year, and Hall was one of three finalists. Before leaving home, a colleague texted, advising Hall to dress to impress. The message only ratcheted up her nerves. Heart pounding and adrenaline pumping, Hall was visibly on edge during first period, watching the door with anticipation. But the first class was uneventful. Partly to calm herself—and partly to improve her view of the school's main entrance—she decided to visit the cosmetology teacher during her planning block.

As Hall walked the hallways to the mock salon she was struck by the stillness, a hunch that something was up. Outside Hall's eyesight, a crowd of school leaders and television cameras were lined up and waiting to enter her classroom. Shortly after, back in room 263, she readied herself for the next class. Suddenly her room was a blur of excitement: other teachers streaming in to catch the moment; scholars confused by the commotion; and the door bursting open, followed by her husband Mardis alongside City Schools CEO Sonja Santelises and Carver staff carrying flowers, balloons, and a framed plaque. LaQuisha Hall was Baltimore's top teacher.

The honor was humbling—her blueprint for student success had earned a citywide accolade. Hall considered herself an avatar for the talented and hardworking teachers throughout Baltimore. The award came with some perks: cash, classroom supplies, and the distinction of throwing the first pitch at a Baltimore Orioles game. It was the notoriety of being an award-winning teacher that ironically led Hall's friends and acquaintances to urge her to leave teaching for school administration. It was a familiar tune, but the chorus grew louder and more insistent after the Teacher of the Year honors.

In public education, the lure to be a school administrator is strong. The transition to administration brings more money and influence over decision- and policy-making. For teachers, becoming a principal is a reliable entryway to leadership. An *Education Week* summary published in 2017 found that nearly all principals start their education career in the classroom. Yet for most teachers, career advancement is not synonymous with pursuing the post of principal. A 2013 national survey by MetLife revealed that more than two-thirds of teachers are not interested in becoming a principal, while more than half are somewhat interested in a hybrid job combining teaching with leadership positions in their school or district.

Redefining how leadership is identified and rewarded in

schools is evolving. According to MetLife, roughly half of teachers serve as department chairs, coaches, and mentors. The year that Hall chaired Forest Park's English department boosted her confidence. It also shifted her view that leadership is tantamount to a management title. It was a different level of accountability, and she felt a duty to all of the English students in the building knowing their English teachers reported to her. She realized taking responsibility for instructional outcomes was transferrable to the classroom.

"There was so much at stake if I were to drop the ball," she says about running a department. "But after leaving that position, I maintained that level of leadership. If I could do that with an entire school, I could do that with a class." While still teaching, Hall has taken online courses in educational leadership that satisfy Maryland's requirement to renew her teaching license every five years. All the while disrupting the long-held assumption that teachers must exit the classroom to feel ambitious and fulfilled.

"If you take all of the good teachers out of the classroom, where are we going to get more good teachers from?" she asks. "Some of us need to stay and be excellent here with kids at the ground level. Everyone doesn't have to be an administrator." She de-emphasizes the impulse to attain a leadership title by practicing daily leadership in the classroom and school.

Helping colleagues understand the significance of mental and emotional wellness in their personal and professional lives is a central passion. At a gathering organized by the Baltimore City Schools human resources division, new and longer-serving teachers listened to Hall explain how to stay centered amidst the chaos that comes with their jobs—be it from difficult students, cantankerous parents, demanding administrators, or overbearing officials. Hall led an art journaling class that combined sketching and sermonizing, as she shared sixteen years of wisdom. "Self-care is not just getting your nails done and doing Reiki. What is stressful in your life . . . what do you need to change?" she posed to the group. "That requires reflection."

A hallmark of her leadership is the willingness to share her concepts and methods with contemporaries. Hall started blogging to great success, with teachers downloading her lesson plans on integrating art and independent reading into the classroom. The blog provides a new medium for Hall to advance teaching as a collaborative enterprise. Photographs of students nationwide engaged in learning activities she conceived have flowed into her email inbox. "I think I got almost eight hundred views when I shared the first link." She beams.

The drive personified by Hall is championed by Santelises, whose "Lead From Your Seat" initiative combats the notion that leadership is connected solely to a high-ranking post. Her résumé includes stints at the nonprofit Education Trust, where she oversaw K–12 policy; in Boston, where she was assistant superintendent for teaching and learning; and in Baltimore, where she served as chief academic officer. Santelises took the helm of Baltimore's schools in July 2016, bringing nearly thirty years of experience in transforming big-city school systems, and was familiar with the stagnation in many school districts.

"Lead From Your Seat" reinterprets the idea of leadership from one's position to one's disposition, prioritizing problem-solving, being proactive, and leading by example. The change was a deliberate move "to get us out of complacency," Santelises says, explaining that when leadership is vested in a person's rank, it can make those in ground-level positions feel powerless. By breaking leadership silos, she aims to redistribute power to low- and mid-level district employees. It has been applied across job categories, with a school secretary offering input on a new phone system, and an office worker troubleshooting and solving a data collection problem. "It's not some noblesse oblige thing," she insists. "My role might be different. I might have different responsibilities and decision-making authority, but it doesn't make me smarter."

Santelises is starting to see her point of view spread across the district as teachers lead professional learning for their colleagues and shift their mindsets. Hall was an early adopter. The chief executive credits her with creating an impressive campaign in November 2018. After two rough weeks of the city's public schools getting beat up in the press, Hall launched #TeamCitySchools, to demonstrate the pride of teachers, principals, parents, and the public in Baltimore's school system. Within forty-eight hours support was widespread, with #TeamCitySchools posts blowing up across Facebook.

Santelises calls Hall's online crusade a manifestation of her philosophy. "She saw that there was an imbalanced narrative, and said, 'I'm not waiting for the news station to change. Doggone it, we're gonna do this!' and she did. My communications team didn't do it. We didn't have a marketing consultant do it. And it was amazing!" The admiration is mutual. Hall recalls prior superintendents who instilled fear in teachers and stifled creativity, and one district administrator who was nonchalant and unmotivated.

Santelises ushered in a new era where teaching beyond the curriculum is encouraged, she says, and "best practices" now delivers meaningful, measurable results for kids. With a wide smile, Hall states that the current CEO has reinvigorated her. "I feel like she gave me permission to be a teacher and a leader at the same time, so I'm taking it full throttle and moving ahead." Having the backing of higher-ups is vital. As the country becomes more polarized, some teachers are retreating from raising controversial issues in the classroom for fear of sparking outrage and its unpredictable outcomes.

Hall exercises leadership by tackling tough subjects with her scholars, despite the landmines. While teaching the story of Emmett Till—a fourteen-year-old Black child tortured and murdered in Mississippi in 1955 in a brutal act of racial violence—class discussion veered off into the use of the N-word within the Black community. An angry parent took her complaints to the principal, demanding that Hall justify her decision. She says the episode reinforced that introducing such material only becomes a dilemma when people outside her classroom make it one. That parent's child returned to class the next day enthusiastic, participatory, and apologetic.

Her students appreciate debating topics that they might not talk over at home, she says. "They see it in the news, and they may not understand it, so when they come to school and hear it from an educator, now they have a better understanding." Protecting the classroom as a safe place for teachers to explore difficult subjects without interference is a tricky affair. What gets labeled as taboo for English class-rooms is highly subjective.

The traditional literary canon is filled with novels featur-ing sex, vulgar language, and even masturbation. But seldom do Orwell's *1984*, Steinbeck's *Of Mice and Men*, or Faulkner's *As I Lay Dying* generate the same uproar as teachers lead-ing constructive conversations on race, racism, immigration, and LGBTQ equality. Case in point: *The Hate U Give*, a YA novel about police violence through the eyes of a sixteen-year-old Black girl, was temporarily banned in 2017 by the Katy Independent School District in Texas. The book was eventually returned to Katy's high school libraries under the condition that librarians inform parents if their child checked out the book, or obtain parental permission in advance.

In room 263 copies of the *New York Times* bestseller are stacked high. The combustible topics of race and politics are regularly discussed in Hall's classroom. Such honest and searching dialogue prepares her scholars for life after high school. She makes a distinction between civics edu-cation and political partisanship, noting that her students should know about voting, elections, the branches of gov-ernment, and the democratic process to be informed and engaged participants in civic life. "I don't have to persuade you to take a certain route, but you should be educated on the routes," she says. "We're producing graduates who don't know the difference between a Democrat and a Republican, so I'm going to tell them when they're in my class."

Her thinking is in step with public school teachers nationally. The 2019 PDK survey revealed 81 percent favor a required civics class, more than the general public (70 percent) and parents (60 percent). Navigating this opinion divide can be challenging, says Paula McAvoy, assistant professor of social studies education at North Carolina State University. In *The Political Classroom: Evidence and Ethics in Democratic Education*, McAvoy and her co-author studied the techniques of high school teachers who effectively introduced political issues into their classrooms. The teachers who were profiled spent extensive time preparing and structuring the student discussions, she says, displaying the initiative of a leader.

"There's education and learning that has to happen before you enter the discussion, to get on some common footing," says McAvoy, stressing that "good and careful judgments" about teaching historical context, current social context, varied interpretations, and evidence of various positions is crucial for discussions to go well. Reminiscent of Hall's Socratic Seminar on the policing of Black youth, McAvoy says that the goal in classroom discussions is not neutrality, but fairness—giving a hearing to all views, with teachers setting norms to prevent the tone from becoming dismissive or divisive. "We want to be aiming for high-level academic talk . . . so teachers need to teach kids how to do that."

These types of classroom experiences are particularly important for youngsters like those in Baltimore, says McAvoy. Her findings show that underserved students arrive to school with less political knowledge than their peers from higher-income homes. She called Hall's decision to distinguish America's two major political parties and their platforms "fantastic and absolutely necessary," as this approach has proven to be time well spent. Students in the research study reported higher levels of class engagement, more interest in following the news and discussing politics outside the classroom, and a broader knowledge of the U.S. political system.

A facet of Hall's leadership and an outcome of her willingness to speak out in the classroom is her resolve to speak up for students. When the local Fox news affiliate reported on the "juveniles" arrested following the Memorial Day incident at Baltimore's Inner Harbor, Hall confronted them on Twitter to report that dozens of Baltimore City students— her freshmen—shared stories of triumph and became published authors earlier that week. Before the holiday weekend was over "31 Baltimore City students publish their first book" was the new headline on the FOX45 Baltimore website. "I guess they got sick of me," she laughs.

Outside of quarreling with the press, her Instagram account with over 6,800 followers showcases Baltimore City students. Some educators are surprised by what they see, asking how Hall was able to get students to read a particular book or complete a specific assignment. The meaning behind the questioning is neither subtle nor surprising. Volumes of research reveal biased assumptions and beliefs about Black students' intellect and potential that exist in the institution of public schooling, with its largely white teacher workforce. A 2016 study found white teachers, when evaluating a Black student's academic future, were less likely to predict the student will graduate high school and less likely to think the student will earn a four-year college degree. White teachers hold lower expectations for Black children than of their white classmates. As a result, Black youth are underrepresented in gifted classes, under-enrolled in honors and Advanced Placement courses, and more likely to be diagnosed as learning disabled.

Hall is constructing a new storyline about Black children in Baltimore—and shifting expectations of what they can do and be in the minds of students and in the minds of the masses. Teacher leadership in its rawest form.

8

THE SYSTEM

The first publicly funded school in the American colonies was founded in 1635. The Boston Latin School, boasting alumni like John Hancock and Samuel Adams, was a secondary school to prepare wealthy young white men for college. Formal schooling then was almost exclusively white, male, and elite. Not until the 1830s did the Common School Movement emerge, with its focus on universal tax-funded education, teacher training, and centralized control of public schools. Educating girls became more prevalent, but teaching enslaved Africans to read or write remained forbidden.

Nearly two centuries later, as a principle, every child in America has the right to a free K–12 education, regardless of race, class, gender, language, sexual orientation, or immigration status. In reality, the fifty-one million students enrolled in U.S. public schools receive wildly inequitable educations, with opportunities and outcomes directly linked to race, socioeconomic, and other demographic characteristics. The quality of public education is also highly influenced by where a child lives—a by-product of funding schools with local tax dollars.

Remarkably, basic components of the one-room schoolhouse era persist: groups of children taught by a single teacher; six-hour school days; and a 180-day school year that dates back to a move in the late 1800s to standardize school calendars nationwide—a compromise between rural areas where kids missed school to harvest crops in the spring and fall, and large cities where year-round schooling was typical. Hall finds the parallels striking. "If you think about why school looks the way it does, it's based off a past that we're no longer living," she says. "There's a whole lot of room for creativity that people aren't considering. We have entrepreneurs making money off YouTube. Why are we still doing things the same way?"

Her question is a familiar critique of public schooling, highlighting the glacial pace of change that characterizes the education sector. School systems are bureaucracies, and at the core of bureaucracy is its organizational structure—a hierarchical model where information and decisions flow from the top down through levels of subordinates. In the administration of schools, superintendents are at the top of the pyramid.

As the chief executive, superintendents steer the educational, operational, and fiscal planning for a school system. In big-city school districts like Baltimore, with a \$1.3 billion operating budget and 168 schools, the job is comparable to running a small town. The vast majority of superintendents are appointed by, and report to, local school boards that enact policies and procedures governing local schools. School superintendents oversee the needs of students and school employees, and balance the concerns of parents, community members, and elected leaders—accountable to all for supervising the day-to-day affairs. The role requires making decisions on curriculum, leading districtwide initiatives that improve student learning, cutting school programs, and canceling school in inclement weather. Reporting typically to the superintendent are assistant or associate superintendents, deputies who direct priorities within the school system, including curriculum and instruction, human resources, special education, and student services, as well as supervise clusters of schools by geographical area or grade level depending on the district's size.

Moving down the pyramid to the school level are principals. As a child, being called to the principal's office is unnerving. In actuality, the job comes with an astounding number of duties apart from disciplining disobedient students: meeting with teaching teams, answering to district leaders, placating parents, and keeping the school's teaching and learning culture front of mind. A 2013 report published by the two national associations representing elementary and secondary school principals found that the position today is a fusion of educational leader, forward thinker, disciplinarian, community builder, and budget analyst who is "expected to broker the often-conflicting interests of parents, teachers, students, district officials, unions, and state and federal agencies."

Assistant principals and department chairs round out school management teams, with teachers and other school staff making up the base of the pyramid. This model has its advantages: clear lines of authority, and specialized roles and responsibilities. Yet as Hall and other teachers can attest, the downsides are plentiful: bureaucratic tiers that stifle innovation and experimentation, and marginalize teachers' voices and autonomy. Teachers want the freedom to take ownership of their classroom and do what's in the best interest of students—how schools are structured and managed creates insurmountable obstacles.

Seeing kids are bored with a book and being allowed to

introduce alternatives is how Hall defines autonomy. She's experienced the opposite, recalling administrators or a department head "walking in and checking to make sure you're on the right day and time in the curriculum, or that you put a certain poster up on a certain wall, in a certain color. That to me is micromanagement." Ascribing to the dictum of Black social historian Lerone Bennett Jr., who stated, "An educator in a system of oppression is either a revolutionary or an oppressor," Hall identifies herself as "One-hundred percent revolutionary." She confesses to struggling with teaching decisions during her career that may have oppressed her kids, such as knowing what works for a unique group of students, but obliged to rigidly follow the district's curriculum. This is a common teacher frustration.

Thomas, Hall's teaching friend, has the trust and backing of her principal at Holabird Academy. Her prior assignment in Baltimore was far more constraining. She's now free to try new ideas in the classroom. Previously the message was "We're going to do it this way and even though it may not be working, we're going to continue to do that." Thomas describes a toxic, draining environment that ignored her experience and insights to the detriment of student learning. In one episode, her students had successfully finished an English unit, and she had advanced to the next skill in the curriculum ahead of schedule. Her supervisor, observing the class, told her to reteach the completed lesson, forcing her to rehash old material.

Similarly, Heffelmire finds Baltimore's high school English curriculum confining. "I don't think it mirrors our students. I don't think it's what we should really be teaching," she says, noting that she supplements the required syllabus with projects and texts she believes are more effective. Scaling up the culturally responsive methods she and Hall advocate requires more than individual teachers embracing this approach. School leaders with an allegiance to culturally responsive school systems are fundamental. Absent this, even self-proclaimed teaching rebels can find themselves hamstrung. Between the extremes of one-size-fits-all teaching mandates and a free-for-all in the classroom lies professional independence that is vital to teacher job satisfaction and longevity. This is particularly true in urban school systems where teacher turnover is high and morale is often low.

Diminished teacher autonomy ranks near the top of systemic factors that undermine good teaching. Coming in a close second is problematic principals—controlling, detached, uninspired. As a new teacher at Edmondson-Westside, Hall was fond of her principal and they built a strong rapport. She remembers another principal who took an interest in the entire staff, and she shined under her direction. Though for most of her seventeen years, encompassing her time at Carver, she's gone unnoticed. While attending to the squeaky wheel and putting out fires is a skill set every principal should possess, too often it becomes their modus operandi. As in any workplace, some employees need more attention, but all employees deserve attention. Encouraging high performers is as essential as identifying and intervening with underperformers.

Hall wants principals to do for teachers what she does for her scholars: "forming those relationships, checking on them, making sure they're okay, making sure they're progressing." In a word, support. As a successful veteran, she reckons her principal assumes she's fine. What this conclusion overlooks is the value of positive feedback and the innate desire of every person to be recognized. "I don't think I'm so much of a star teacher, I just think that [students] appreciate going into a class where the teacher is on their feet, walking around, having discussions with them," she says, rejecting the superstar title. "It would be nice to have her come see some of the cool things I'm doing in class." Instead, Hall says the recurring pattern is administrators appearing "when people outside of the school show interest," showering her with praise for TV cameras and special guests.

Most of all, she would love for her principal to see the student engagement in her classroom. Chatting with peers, Hall hears a lot of negativity about her kids. She reasons that seeing students shining who regularly get a bad rap would give the principal a more balanced view on Carver's teens. But her wish remains unfulfilled. Even in the best circumstances, keeping teachers motivated can be challenging, and scarce acknowledgment is fuel to the fire. The actions of school administrators, coupled with curriculum choices and school finance decisions, are the bureaucratic forces that impede quality teaching.

Casting a spotlight on chronic funding shortfalls is especially illuminating. In 2016–17, the most recent year for which federal data is available, $739 billion in local, state, and federal tax dollars was spent on public education. By comparison, a July 2016 analysis from the U.S. Education Department found state and local spending on prisons and jails far outpaced funding for preschool through grade 12, with corrections budgets increasing at triple the rate of public education spending in the last three decades. According to the National Center for Education Statistics, roughly 80 percent of school spending was allocated to district employees' salaries and benefits; 11 percent to professional development for teachers and food, custodial, and transportation services; 7 percent to supplies ranging from books to heating oil; and the remaining 2 percent to other expenditures.

Nationwide, an average of $12,201 was spent per public school student, with Baltimore City ranking third among the one hundred largest school districts at $16,184 per pupil based on 2017 Census data. Looking at raw dollar amounts, however, is misleading with the rising costs of special education, more students in poverty, unfunded state mandates, and other budgetary demands. In the latest PDK Poll on attitudes toward public schools, a large share of the general public believe schools are inadequately funded. Six in ten parents and other adults—and seven in ten Black poll respondents—say public schools in their community have too little money. Three-quarters (75 percent) of teachers say local schools are underfunded. And among well-off households making $100,000-plus, presumably in communities with already well-funded schools, a majority (54 percent) say their schools need more resources.

How much money is enough is a perennial point of dispute, with state legislatures and governors crafting education budgets. Contrary to popular belief, federal spending is less than ten cents—some 8 percent—of every dollar spent on the nation's public schools. The primary sources of public education revenue are state sales, income, and other taxes, and local property taxes—resulting in wide disparities between wealthy and impoverished communities and their schools. As school financing debates rage on, teachers contend that what matters is the amount of money that is funneled to the school and classroom level. Over the years Thomas has seen schools decimate arts, music, and sports programs, citing funding shortages. Sounding nostalgic, she attended a Title I school in Los Angeles that "always had a librarian, and we also had an actual library with books you could check out." School librarians are becoming "the unicorns of education," she states, referring to their declining numbers amid tightened school budgets. "That's part of literacy; you need that. So if you can't get funding for simple things . . . that's a problem."

Reflecting on her first years of teaching, Heffelmire says "tangible resources" are linked to how teachers rate a school's environment. "Imagine walking into a building that is freezing cold or too hot, where you don't have toilet paper, or soap to wash your hands," she says, describing her former high school, where to get printer paper "we almost had to Hunger Games for it." More than an inconvenience, it was dehumanizing for students. "That's what they're being told education is. 'Here's how much we care about you. This is what we're giving you. This is how important you are.'" Carver is a great school, she says, not because the school is "super-unique" but the basics are covered, so she can concentrate on teaching.

The conditions that Heffelmire faced are the subject of a decades-old ACLU of Maryland lawsuit suing the state over its "unconstitutional and inequitable" funding of Baltimore City Schools, spanning generations of schoolchildren. The 1994 *Bradford v. Maryland State Board of Education* case led to revamping the statewide school funding formula in 2002. Now plaintiffs have filed to reopen the *Bradford* lawsuit, arguing that Maryland lawmakers continue to short-change Baltimore's public school students. One estimate put the shortfall at over $2 billion in constitutionally required funding. Civil rights groups explicitly slammed Maryland leaders for the abysmal physical state of Baltimore's school facilities. City Schools made headlines in 2018 for alternating bouts of extreme cold that closed schools for days in January, and stifling heat in classrooms that sent kids home early in September. In room 263, the air-conditioning unit is running full blast on a June morning, a few of Hall's scholars complaining of the chill. Hall jokingly reminds them that not long ago they were grumbling about sweating from the heat.

Most of the schools she's worked in were aging buildings with temperamental heating and cooling systems. True to her nature, she looked for solutions, bringing a portable heater or a fan, as needed. "I am a problem solver by nature," she says. "I don't complain. I adjust." The key question is, at what cost? The expectation that teachers will accept subpar conditions related to their work "for the kids" is pervasive and uniquely connected to the system of schooling. Hospital systems don't expect nurses to purchase bandages for their patients. The court system doesn't require stenographers to supply their own paper. It speaks to how state leaders and policymakers value the skilled professionals who educate their community's children that they would ask them to teach in sweltering or freezing classrooms.

Problems run deeper than that. Doris Santoro, professor of education at Bowdoin College, says institutional factors in public schooling make it extremely hard for teachers to do good work. Her 2018 book, *Demoralized: Why Teachers Leave the Profession They Love and How They Can Stay*, profiles twenty-three experienced teachers who remained in the classroom despite profound discontent. Originally she set out to study experienced teachers who leave. This sparked her interest in better understanding why some stay. Santoro's research identifies reasons teachers become demoralized, among them standardized testing, scripted curriculum, and the constant cycle of new school system initiatives. Conversely, the major factor keeping them in the classroom is caring, constructive professional learning communities online and in-person. In a word, support.

In spite of the tendency to label dissatisfied veterans as ready to retire, they are anything but, she says. The teachers Santoro interviewed "have plenty to offer. They just feel like they're not able to give it, that there's no space for them to contribute in the way that they believe is correct for the profession . . . or what kids deserve." For good teaching to prosper, some basic rules apply: respect teacher expertise, ask teachers what they need to do their best work and what gets in the way, and give teachers opportunities to improve their practice and grow. Demoralization is not just being bummed out or unhappy, but "literally being unable to access what makes your job good," Santoro explains, upending the conventional teacher burnout narrative. What she articulates resonates with Hall, who recalls a recent conversation with Carver's principal that left her dejected.

The point of contention was an end-of-year field trip. When her freshmen were invited to participate in a student pen-pal project, Hall jumped at the chance for her kids to mentor fifth-graders from Thomas Johnson Elementary/ Middle School in Baltimore's predominantly white Federal Hill neighborhood. In a city divided by race and income, she wanted the younger children to see her West Baltimore kids "for who they are. People just like them . . . I wanted them to read a note from one of my students and say, 'Wow, this guy is cool' or 'This young lady reads the same books that I do.'" To culminate the writing activity, Hall's scholars planned to visit the middle-school students in June. Until getting the student permission slip initialed by her principal became an inexplicable tug-of-war.

"She wouldn't approve it initially. And I've been on twenty field trips this year for my kids," she recounts. "She gave me a hard time in the office . . . 'Why didn't I get this two weeks in advance?' 'I've got to talk to our financial office.' All I needed was her permission. I had it from there."

At 12:40 p.m., the day before the field trip, Hall was summoned to the front office to get the signed form. Exasperated, she scrambled to distribute the permission slips through student word-of-mouth, and a last-minute announcement on the loudspeaker before the day ended. Huddled in her doorway, she handed out slips and pleaded with students to have the forms signed overnight and returned. The following day Mrs. Hall and her scholars boarded the bus to spend the day with their pen pals in South Baltimore.

In well-functioning schools, teacher collaboration is

encouraged, not hindered, Santoro counsels. In well-functioning school systems, various parts work in unison to support the greater good: in this case, student well-being and learning. Hall's case study in the administrative bureaucracy of schools is an omen. With all of the challenges that public school systems face in the twenty-first century, addressing teacher demoralization may be the most urgent.

9

BLACK TEACHERS MATTER

"Jeremiah" looks flustered and ready to give up. "Can I just write a paragraph?" Clustered in groups of three or four, Hall's scholars read two-sided flashcards on lesser-known Black history and are asked to create a single page—with text and drawings—analyzing the historical and contemporary relevance of their person or event. The assignment combats an all-too-often whitewashed version of history that erases the contributions of Black Americans. The stuck student isn't feeling very imaginative as Hall walks the room, checking in with youngsters. Two boys sit on bean bag chairs between the bookcases. Like a ninja, she can tell they're doing more than schoolwork on their phones. Speaking to no one in particular, but loud enough for everyone to hear, she reminds the class that phones are for internet research, not Instagram.

Hall is omnipresent as her students jot facts and thoughts

about Angela Davis, Marcus Garvey, Black Wall Street, Malcolm X, and Nina Simone, among others. Jeremiah is assigned legendary gold medal track-and-field athlete Jesse Owens, and is struggling to think creatively. With encouragement from Hall, he picks up an Arizona Iced Tea and begins tracing overlapping circles to illustrate the Olympic rings. She gives him a slight grin. He meets her gaze with a nod and continues working to meet the end-of-class deadline. Hall coaxing a student to move beyond what's comfortable is nothing new. What makes the moment atypical is that it's a Black teacher guiding a Black child to find his creative fire. The average public school teacher looks nothing like Hall.

Nationally, Black teachers are a meager portion (7 percent) of the teacher workforce—fewer than one in ten—while federal data shows eight out of ten teachers are white, a noted trend that has endured for decades. The teaching profession is considerably whiter than the student population in public schools, where 49 percent of kids are white, and the nation at large, where 61 percent of Americans identify as white. The upshot is classrooms filled with a diverse student body, and few teachers who share their racial and cultural heritage.

The causes of the Black teacher shortage are easier to list than solve. Barriers to diversifying teaching include licensure exams that disproportionately exclude Black teacher candidates, racial discrimination in school-district hiring, inadequate support for new teachers, and displacement due to reorganizing and closing high-needs, under-resourced schools where Black teachers are concentrated.

For the Black teachers who persevere, the rewards outweigh the obstacles. In Baltimore County, Penn always had a passion for working with children, which led him to the classroom. He is triply rare—Black, male, and an elementary teacher. Less than 2 percent of the nation's public school teachers are Black men. While studying to be a teacher at Long Island University in New York, Penn worked at a local high school. It cemented his desire to help fill the void of Black men who teach in the early grades. "I realized that once a student is sixteen to eighteen years old, their personality has really molded . . . to build that foundation and instill a love of learning, you need to attack it when they are four to seven years old." Out of the gate, Penn found himself pigeonholed as the disciplinarian, responsible for misbehaving students in his and his colleagues' classes. The practice is so common that researchers have analyzed its effect, finding that typecasting Black teachers as disciplinarians for Black children—and asking them to serve as "veritable parents within educational settings"—leads to "scores of exceedingly qualified educators willing to [assist], but also overburdened and sometimes disillusioned with the additional duties."

Tasked with this role in his first couple years teaching, Penn resigned himself once the import of his presence sunk in. Accounts from parents pointed to the invaluable role Black teachers play in bolstering Black students' academic motivation and sense of belonging. Handling disciplinary issues became an opportunity instead of a burden when Penn realized his positive influence on students. "I wanted to be that example for kindergartners and first-grade students that, 'Wow, there's an intelligent, proud Black man . . . and

I learned a lot from him.' I wanted to be able to provide that experience."

Like Penn, Thomas symbolizes the scarcity of Black teachers, noting that she was the only Black woman at Holabird Academy in the 2018 school year. Her journey into teaching was a bit of a fluke. In college she enrolled in an education class when the electives she wanted were filled. She continued taking education classes and was smitten. "It was not in the plan ever. But I'm very happy to be here." Thomas says there is a deliberate level of care that Black teachers convey that exceeds teaching the traditional three Rs of reading, writing, and arithmetic. In her current school, where the majority of the teaching staff is white, she is a role model, mentor, and champion for Black and Latinx children's potential. "My expectations are high. I'm going to hold your feet to the fire, but I'm also going to love on you at the same time to make sure you're able to meet those goals," Thomas says, referencing the racially biased judgments some teachers hold about children's capabilities. "In a cultural way, I think it's very important for students to see someone who looks like them."

Thomas is also an asset to non-Black children in her school. She refuses to shy away from the realities of racism and discrimination in the subjects they discuss in her class.

"Those conversations may be hard, but they need to be had. I'm not going to present this lopsided view to make things seem like they're perfect or paint history as if it's all positive. I want them to hear other people's stories." Those lessons extend to colleagues. Black teachers must navigate the "outsider" dynamic when working in majority-white schools. Thomas recalls having to educate a coworker who sympathized with the Confederacy and those flying the Confederate flag. After coming under fire, the colleague explained that the remark was misinterpreted. Thomas responded that it was an unacceptable comment in front of "someone who is Black and who has ancestors who were enslaved people," signaling that her Blackness is nonnegotiable.

Heffelmire seconds this point of view. Her identity as a multiracial Black woman is embedded in everything she teaches. In her high school classroom, *The Crucible*—a dramatized story of the Salem witch trials—is shelved in favor of *No Choirboy: Murder, Violence, and Teenagers on Death Row*, an intense portrait of America's system of juvenile punishment. She entered teaching believing she was more than an English instructor—that her role was to give Black students "the specific skills that they need to go out in a society that is working to oppress them, where racism is so prevalent and real." Black teachers are more suitable to deliver this message, she says, because students can see themselves in their teachers. She affectionately recalls her lone Black teacher from elementary through high school, Mr. Green: "I'll always remember him. You have to think as a little Black girl sitting in a classroom . . . and you're never taught by someone that looks like you, and what that does. Black teachers are so important. We're so necessary."

Her belief is borne out by research on the long-term gains Black students obtain from Black teachers. In 2017 researchers from Johns Hopkins University and American University reported that Black students who have at least one Black teacher in elementary school are more likely to graduate high school than those who don't. A single Black teacher reduced the prospect of a Black student dropping out by 29 percent, and for Black boys, their likelihood of becoming a dropout fell by 39 percent. A 2018 paper by the same research team went further, concluding that one Black teacher in elementary school not only improves a Black child's probability of earning a high school diploma, but makes them 13 percent more likely to enroll in college than peers without any Black teachers. Black youngsters with a Black kindergarten teacher were as much as 18 percent more likely to enroll in college—and kids with two Black teachers were 32 percent more likely to go to college.

Even with evidence of the benefits of Black teachers, school systems continue to struggle to find and keep teachers like Hall, Heffelmire, Thomas, and Penn. The negative perception of the children Baltimore's public schools serve is the crux of the local problem, says Hall. She often finds herself refuting the low opinion of Black children to Black adults who "talk about how terrible our kids are." Part of her rationale for sharing the good news in Baltimore schools is that she believes disparaging Black kids unintentionally discourages Black candidates from coming into the profession, and deters Black teachers from working in her district. Penn cosigns the idea of swapping negative stories about teaching and unruly children with examples of the impact Black teachers have "on a community, on a classroom, on a kid."

Thomas pinpoints the lack of cultural support for Black teachers to navigate the implicit biases they encounter. For instance, having a white teacher touch their natural hair—a situation that happened to her. After texting Hall for advice on how to handle that, the nine-year teaching veteran was firm in telling her colleague why it was inappropriate. "If that's a first-year teacher having to deal with that, and not necessarily having anyone to turn to and talk to, that would get difficult." Thomas also repeats the refrain of teacher pay, citing Black teachers who have left the profession "because they weren't paid enough and they needed money to pay bills. And they didn't want to have to work multiple jobs to do that."

Confronted with a dismal record of hiring and keeping Black teachers, Baltimore City Schools formed a group to address the barriers to recruitment and retention. Their June 2019 report cited the research on the effect of Black teachers on Black students' academic success, and high-lighted the disparity between the city's Black teaching force (45 percent) and its Black student population (nearly 80 percent). The assessment was blunt: "A contributing factor in the decline of the number of Black teachers teaching in our schools is systemic racism . . . at every phase, including pathways into teaching, certification requirements, mentoring experiences, and working conditions." Or maybe the answer is as basic, yet elusive, as recognizing and rewarding the strengths and contributions of Black teachers. "Once those Black teachers come in, how do we get them to stay?" Hall ponders. "The amount of work . . . the way they might be treated by school administration. They are quick to leave because they don't feel appreciated."

She also asserts that not all Black teachers have the mindset to effectively teach Black kids. She depicts mostly-Black schools in Baltimore with same-race teachers who recklessly wield their authority. "I have seen Black teachers say, 'You're going to follow my rules and what I say. I'm the teacher. I'm in charge.' That's how unfortunately a lot of us are raised. 'Speak when spoken to, or stay in a child's place.'" In contrast, Hall says her scholars frequently push the boundaries, as teens are wont to do. Rather than scold them, she extends leniency. Oftentimes they ask to step into the hallway to take phone calls from home, knowing it's forbidden during class. "They know that they have to read. They know what I require as a teacher . . . I think my relationship with students is even better because they knew that I wasn't going to penalize them for that."

Hall's observations underscore that the drive for more Black teachers needs an asterisk. Melanin in the skin is not a proxy for bringing a caring, or culturally responsive, approach to teaching. Building connections with Black children and doing "whatever it takes to reach the students" is not innate but learned, Hall says. The same way white teachers need training to develop positive, respectful relationships with Black youngsters, Black teachers need guidance to acquire these skills. When that happens, what Black teachers bring to the classroom is inarguably special. "When they look at us, they see what's possible," Hall says, emphasizing the power of representation. "When you are

Black, you know what Black people experience, what they go through . . . kids connect to that in a different way when it comes to Black teachers, because they see it as, 'My teacher's trying to help me because I'm like them.'"

In fact, Black teachers are preferred by students of all races. A provocative 2016 study from Hua-Yu Sebastian Cherng, a sociologist at New York University's Steinhardt School, scrutinized data on students' opinions of their teachers. More than fifty thousand middle- and high school students in two hundred urban schools were asked to rate their teachers on how well they explain difficult concepts, whether they make the class interesting, and other measures of the classroom experience. He found that students, regardless of their race and ethnicity, perceived Black teachers—more than their white peers—"to hold students to high academic standards and support their efforts, to help them organize content, and to explain ideas clearly and provide feedback." Asian American students favored Black teachers more highly than did Black youth.

Hall believes the preference for Black teachers is note-worthy. "It's important for young people to grow up having a Black teacher, hearing from an African American who is college educated and professional," she says, given the pervasive one-sided portrayals of Black life in the media and society. "I think it helps to have them experience that hands-on." Though she confesses that her methods would differ in a predominantly white classroom. "Honestly, if I taught white students, I'd probably stick to the curriculum," she admits. In teaching Black students almost exclusively, her approach is not just educating them but advocating for them. Remembering the lesson on the Inner Harbor incident, she says that conversation was more poignant because her scholars were directly affected. "I felt that my students could have possibly been a part of that whole debacle," Hall says, and due to that reality "it was best to educate them on being conscientious of where they are and who they're with."

Teaching in West Baltimore is where she thrives—and where she knows the pool of future Black teachers exists. Hall regularly talks to her kids about their interest in teaching, answering questions about why she became a teacher and how long she's been at it. Many of them have heard the negative rhetoric about her profession, and counter that with the positive impact she has made in their lives. As the school year ends, she has one student who is dead set on following in her footsteps. "I want to be an elementary school teacher," she tells her. Exemplifying the adage of "each one reach one."

10

CLEAN SLATE

The annual ritual known as back-to-school is a frantic time for kids and parents—whether finishing summer assignments or stocking up on school supplies. Similarly, teachers are busy in the days leading up to a new school year. Hall is animated on an unseasonably mild August day. During the summer she visualized the cosmetic changes she wanted to make to her classroom. Now she's a burst of energy as the finishing touches are applied. Entering room 263, the renovation is striking. One wall is painted fuchsia; the opposite wall is black and white stripes. The colorful spines of brand-new YA books complement the teal and yellow bookcases, with *The Prince and the Dressmaker*, *Ghost Boys*, and *Barely Missing Everything* among this year's selections. Tucked away in a corner is a Zen-like reading nook, a small pile of books stacked neatly next to a wicker chair.

Centered in the room is the masterpiece: a prominent seating area for the "scholar of the week and friends" featuring a stylish table, sleek upholstered chairs, a striped plush rug, and decorative faux chandeliers overhead. Hall spent months bringing her vision to life, and she is excited for the unveiling. As an artist, she enjoys working in a visually pleasing environment. But this makeover, upwards of $2,500, is essentially to make her scholars feel extra special. "When my kids walk to school and all they see is dilapidated buildings and people standing on the corner . . .

I wanted to create something inside my classroom that was pleasant for them," she says boldly, rebuffing naysayers who question her investment in the showpiece room.

Hall has taught English 1 to many incoming high schoolers with anxieties about reading. The tranquil space communicates that her classroom is an inviting place where support is abundant. Her goal is to give them an "atmosphere of peace and safety inside a society and a world that's chaotic, [and] where they can feel comfortable learning." The logistical preparations are just one pin that Hall is juggling with Carver reopening. Administrative demands are part of the job. Like the "First Day of School Classroom Readiness Checklist" that administrators will use to confirm that the seventeen-year veteran's bulletin boards are decorated, counters are clutter-free, the bell schedule is posted, and other perfunctory duties are completed before kids arrive.

Inevitably, unexpected changes come up in teacher meetings before the year starts. Hall is cautious, knowing the chasm that exists between intent and implementation. What was formerly the English hallway was refashioned into a dedicated ninth-grade wing. Overflowing bins line the hall as ninth-grade teachers relocate to new classrooms. Hall sees the benefits of separating Carver's newcomers.

"Sometimes our freshmen are trying so hard to fit in with the upperclassmen, they forget why they came here."

Besides the reshuffling, she learns that a new district initiative is launching to track ninth-graders through their high school years, to identify students' post-secondary goals and boost on-time graduation rates. The first year of high school, a huge social and emotional transition, has been proven to be a pivotal year in a student's long-term academic success. Strategies that keep ninth-graders from losing interest and dropping out are critical. At Carver, the four-year dropout rate in 2018 was 9 percent, notably below the district's 15 percent dropout rate. "Entering high school should look like the long stretch to the finish line, but to some kids it looks so far away," she says. "It's important for me to remind them that they can make it . . . that in itself can motivate them to try to go to the next grade level."

What seems to be missing from the pre-year hoopla is any attention to teachers' spirits. The orderly classroom dictated by the checklist might be staffed by a teacher who's fraying at the seams. Hall admits it's an overlooked part of the back-to-school routine. "I guess they feel we're adults, we need to handle that on our own," she concedes. But with a districtwide focus on student wholeness, the irony is hard to miss. "If I'm not socially, emotionally sound, how can

I help a student? I do think that needs to be embedded, but . . . there is no space for that."

Hall vows to maintain her peace in spite of it all. She started yoga over the summer. She reminded Mardis to refill her vitamins. And she cut back on Mountain Dew, her go-to on stressful occasions. "I'm trying to do things that will put my energy levels at a higher place," she says. She has prepared for the first weeks of the year—fully realizing that as it progresses, the stress-free regimen is at risk. "All of these reports and 'Don't forget this paperwork' . . . that's when I start drinking soda like crazy." For now, her outlook is upbeat. "I'm going to keep doing what I need to do [for] kids they put in my class," she declares, noting that after transforming her classroom, "Clearly I'm not leaving for a long time."

CHEAT ON YOUR CELL PHONE EVERY ONCE IN A WHILE WITH A BOOK reads the calligraphed sign that greets Hall's three classes of English 1 and one class of English 3—the juniors are the same group she taught their freshman year. Differentiating content for the two grade levels will mean additional preparation. Even so, having the upperclassmen return to room 263 is one of the joys of this newly minted year. On the first day her freshmen are wowed. One group of youngsters enters, looks around puzzled, waiting for Hall to tell them they can sit. Once the freshmen loosen up, they quickly feel at home. The older students, the majority of whom follow her Instagram, saw preview pictures and are impressed. "It made me feel good to know they appreciated it," she says. "I have a freshman last period that often tells me . . . he's tired all day, but when he comes in here, he just perks up."

Outside of the remodel, the first week is intensely impactful. Hall reads a letter that she's written to the new crop of students as part of a bonding exercise. In it she discloses the personal and the profound: that she's been on her own since sixteen, that she gets sleepy when she reads for too long, and that she expects every scholar to pass her class—a realistic goal with her helping them every step of the way. When asked which of Mrs. Hall's revelations was most surprising, students repeatedly cite her sincere desire to see them do well in school. With Hall's letter serving as a model, students are asked to write a private letter to her in return. The responses are so honest that she's unable to read them all in one sitting.

Scholars reveal they are houseless, and want to help those without permanent housing. One student has developed trichotillomania—the uncontrollable urge to pull out her own hair—after her father was incarcerated. Another lost both parents just a year apart and articulates how the trauma left them feeling emotionally detached. Without knowing her well enough to be sure she was trustworthy, her scholars gave Hall the opportunity to be trusted. Although the letters are emotionally overwhelming, they are the highlight of her week—the key to establishing a new classroom climate that is caring and mutually supportive.

In the coming weeks, that sense of community is solidified as she introduces yoga and restorative circles to her students. Hall was compelled to use the skills in her classroom after a weeklong workshop she took in the summer. She found a sponsor to purchase yoga mats, and contracted with a yogi to lead the sessions for $250 a month. The visits are a hit—one young lady is sleeping better from stretching before bed, and a classmate used deep breathing to calm herself in a heated disagreement. Hall also initiated a restorative practice she calls "Circle Up." She read up on the method, which honors students' experiences of disconnection or alienation, and prioritizes healing at the interpersonal level, emulating customs of Native American, First Nation, and other Indigenous peoples. About 42 percent of K–12 public schools reported holding restorative circles in 2017–18, an increase of 8 percent from 2015–16, according to the research arm of the U.S. Education Department.

Seated in a large circle, Hall's students are silly at first, armed with a plush strawberry pillow as the "talking piece." Finally a young lady opens up, and others follow her lead. Hall is gratified with the outcome as her scholars find their rhythm. Circle Up has become a welcomed weekly routine—a renewing way for students to connect and end the week on Fridays. But the kickoff to the new school year is more than a string of high points. Hall is also confronted with unpleasant moments. As sunshine streams through the window in mid-September, her mood is low. Administrators, conducting a walk-through, recently came into her classroom, requesting to see her lesson plan. She presented an illustrated and laminated sheet of paper with the objective, materials, and tasks for students to complete, as regulations require. Dissatisfied with the presentation, they humiliated Hall, talking within kids' earshot. She later hears that a neighboring teacher's three stapled pages is the preferred format.

The disrespect stings. But the pride she draws from teaching is larger than any single episode. After seventeen years, averaging at least one hundred kids a year, she's taught 1,700 students in Baltimore. Through her "they had the opportunity to be successful educationally, and that's the power of a teacher," she says assertively. Just that week, a ninth-grader she taught some twelve years ago reached out to her. He didn't finish high school, but he follows her on social media, saw her posts about education, and private messaged her seeking help on obtaining his GED. "He was a good kid. He just got caught up in the wrong crowd," she recalls. "He was a great student for me . . . now he's raising his hand, so to speak, to say, 'Can you still help me?'" Of course the answer was yes.

Hall immediately jumped on the phone and directed the young man to free resources. Presently, he's en route to getting his GED and a commercial driver's license that will permit him to do long-haul trucking. She is reflective—and insightful—about watching him blossom more than ten years after dropping out. "Sometimes teachers want kids to understand right then how important education is, but life has to take them on a journey. And if you really are what you say you are, the kids will know how to come back to you . . . they'll return, kind of like a butterfly."

Hall recognized her former student's aspiration to grow, personally and professionally, because the same flame flickers inside her. Teaching is a life-changing endeavor. She has encouraged, loved, and believed in youngsters often before they believed in themselves. Every interaction with her scholars has altered the contours of their lives and helped shape their futures. Those moments have also changed her immeasurably. Hall has drawn strength and sustenance from putting Mrs. Hall's queens and kings forever on a different course. But alas, as the saying goes, you can't pour from an empty vessel. Rewarding as teaching is—and could continue to be—doing the job for almost twenty years can be draining.

Reflecting this truth, Hall stayed home for three days in the first quarter of the school year to do administrative paperwork—refusing to give her scholars worksheets while she completed forms during class time. "I think we should be working together anytime I'm in the classroom," she says. "So to prevent them from feeling like I was disengaged, I took off work to do all these tasks . . . that all had a different acronym . . . that had absolutely nothing to do with them being successful."

As much as people applaud Hall for all she does to extend the curriculum, it's not what her supervisors are evaluating and judging. The checklist has superseded creating excitement in the classroom. "I don't care so much about how people see me as a teacher . . . [If] I can demonstrate that my kids are learning, I feel that should be sufficient." Instead, she fills out papers "just to maintain my job . . . I'm tired of always having to prove myself." Like a game of Jenga, with pieces continually pulled out and placed on top, eventually the tower will implode.

After deep consideration, Hall made the difficult decision that she would permanently exit room 263 at Carver Vo-Tech, and leave full-time teaching in Baltimore public schools. On the cusp of a new decade, she is evolving as an educator and feels pulled to teach and educate in impactful ways outside the classroom. "I know that I still want to be a voice for students, for young people. I know that I still want to see students like the ones that I've been teaching for [nearly] two decades succeed, and that they need a unique voice." Hall's identity as a teacher has always been defined by working hands-on with Black youth. As she moves into uncharted territory, she aspires to redefine what it means to teach and effect change in education. "I'm starting to feel like maybe I need to try this on a larger scale . . . while that 1,700 sounds like a big number, and it is, it could be that times ten (or a hundred)."

She knows that she will forever be connected to her scholars. When the time comes to announce the news, Hall will tell them change is good, and that life won't always look exactly the way you hope, but that's no reason to feel hopeless—exhibiting the clear thinking and open heart that made her a master teacher. She won't be in the classroom, and it won't look the same, but Mrs. Hall will always be their teacher. "I will still be available to support them through school . . . encouraging them to stay focused on their goal of graduating from high school."

Should any of her scholars invite Hall to their high school commencement, she will be there. Guaranteed. "I really want the best for all the kids that I've ever taught."

RESOURCES

Resources Toolkit for New Teachers, *Edutopia*
An array of resources, tips, and advice for teachers just starting out. https://www.edutopia.org/article/new-teacher-resources-toolkit

The *Praxis*® Tests, Educational Testing Service
https://www.ets.org/praxis/

The New Teacher Project (TNTP) Blog
Ideas, research, and opinions on supporting great teaching and creating vibrant classrooms.
https://tntp.org/blog

The PDK Poll of the Public's Attitudes Toward the Public Schools (2019), *Kappan* magazine
https://pdkpoll.org/

Seven Trends: The Transformation of the Teaching Force—Updated October 2018, *CPRE Research Reports*
https://repository.upenn.edu/cgi/viewcontent.cgi?article=1109&context=cpre_researchreports

FURTHER READING

Why Are All the Black Kids Sitting Together in the Cafeteria? And Other Conversations About Race (Basic Books, 2017)
by Beverly Daniel Tatum, PhD
Brings clarity and focus to the concepts of racial identity and the role of race in the classroom. An easy, stimulating read that offers teachers a roadmap to communicating effectively about race, culture, and racism.

The Teacher Wars: A History of America's Most Embattled Profession (Doubleday, 2014)
by Dana Goldstein
An exhaustive history of public school teaching covering nearly two centuries—from the feminization of the teacher workforce in the early nineteenth century, to ways to increase race and gender diversity in the profession today.

Other People's Children: Cultural Conflict in the Classroom (The
    New Press, 2006)
    by Lisa Delpit
    Reveals how the critical factors of race, culture,
    power, and privilege interplay in classrooms between
    predominantly white teachers and "other people's
    children"—namely, children of color. Challenges teachers
    to disrupt the stereotypes, prejudice, and cultural
    assumptions that result in educational inequities.

ABOUT THE AUTHOR

Melinda D. Anderson is a freelance journalist whose reporting brings context to the complicated and critical issues of race and equity in education. Her storytelling champions the voices and perspectives of educators and youth of color. She started her writing career as a freelance reporter for *The Philadelphia Inquirer*, producing feature articles for the lifestyle section. Her most memorable assignment was spending the night in the Franklin Institute, one of the nation's oldest science museums. Melinda currently serves as a contributing writer for *The Atlantic*. She is also a regular contributor to *Edutopia*, the leading magazine for educators illuminating and showcasing what works in education. Her byline has appeared in *The Washington Post*, *Slate*, and other news and magazine outlets.